"*Prayers for Prodigals* sits on my nightstand, and my wife and I have used it often. Few books have ministered to me so personally and have impacted my prayer life so profoundly as this one. *Prayers for Prodigals* is a treasure to any who know or have a prodigal (or any teenager!) and will help you come before your heavenly Father daily, praying the promises of God for your children back to Him."

—**J.D. GREEAR,** pastor, The Summit Church,
Raleigh-Durham, NC, and author of *Just Ask*

"This book will meet a real need for the many parents of prodigals who long to pray their children home and experience God's peace while they're waiting."

—**CHERI FULLER,** speaker and author of *Mother-Daughter Duet* and
The One Year Women's Friendship Devotional

"I am thrilled that this book has been written. Parents of prodigals need so much encouragement to keep praying even when they don't see any evidence of the answer."

—**FERN NICHOLS,** founder, Moms in Prayer International

"My mother, Ruth Bell Graham, would have loved this book. Why? Because she loved prodigals; I know—I was one. James Banks certainly captures the hearts of many mothers and fathers who agonize over wayward children. Even for children who don't walk the prodigal path, all children, teenagers, and adult children need prayer. This book puts such prayer into proper perspective—James has shared from the depth of experience the secret of parental prayers for children and reveals the truth for effective prayer: God's Word. He looks inward first to his own shortfall so that God can then lead him to touch the heart of a loving heavenly Father as he seeks the mind of Christ. I believe if every parent would peruse these pages they would find guidance and comfort in trusting the Lord with their dearest possessions."

—**FRANKLIN GRAHAM**, president and CEO,
Billy Graham Evangelistic Association and Samaritan's Purse

T0109665

"*Prayers for Prodigals* is rooted in Scripture and written with the empathy of someone who understands how you feel. If you are a parent who is brokenhearted, hopeless, and desperate, this book will be a gift for you. If you feel like you don't even have the words or energy to pray, these pages will be a trusted and compassionate guide."

—**DREW HILL,** award-winning author of *Alongside: Loving Teenagers with the Gospel*

"James has experienced the heartache of a child who has not just walked away from faith in God but seemingly abandoned life itself. His story grabs at my heart. For I too have known the wrenching pain of praying for prodigals to return. As thousands and thousands have read, *Prayers for Prodigals* offers prayerful encouragement and hope—real hope—to those who are in the middle of those prodigal stories."

—**ELISA MORGAN,** author, speaker,
and cohost of *God Hears Her* and *Discover the Word*

"Years of pastoring and counseling have brought many parents my way who have wayward children. Our God, who answers prayer, is the key in children returning to God and to their parents. I look forward to using this resource to help many hurting parents!"

—**DR. KERRY L. SKINNER,** president and cofounder, Think LifeChange

"James Banks is a dear brother and colleague who has more passion for the subject of prayer than anyone I have ever known. He has also experienced the heartache of prodigal kids and knows how that can drive you to your knees. I could not recommend James more highly, especially when he is dealing with subjects so close to his heart. I pray that you will find hope, encouragement, and wisdom as you seek the God of rescue and experience the blessing and power of prayer through James's ministry."

—**BILL CROWDER,** Bible teacher, Our Daily Bread Ministries, and
cohost of *Discover the Word* podcast

"As a father and grandfather, I have sometimes searched hard for words to express both gratitude and longing for our young ones. I find James Banks's words of prayer honest and helpful, and have already shared them with my grown children for their own use!"

—**LEIGHTON FORD,** president, Leighton Ford Ministries

Prayers for Prodigals

90 DAYS of PRAYER for YOUR CHILD

Updated and Expanded

James Banks

Our Daily Bread
Publishing®

Requests for permission to quote from this book should be directed to: Permissions
Department, Our Daily Bread Publishing, PO Box 3566, Grand Rapids, MI 49501,
or contact us by email at permissionsdept@odb.org.

Library of Congress Cataloging-in-Publication Data
Names: Banks, James, author.
Title: Prayers for prodigals : 90 days of prayer for your child / James Banks.
Description: Grand Rapids : Our Daily Bread Publishing, [2022] | Includes bibliographical references
    and index. | Summary: "This unique book inspires parents to maintain a sustained, daily prayer effort
    for their prodigal children, especially when they feel tired and discouraged"-- Provided by publisher.
Identifiers: LCCN 2021045636 | ISBN 9781640701403 (paperback)
Subjects: LCSH: Parents of problem children--Religious life. | Intercessory prayer--Christianity. |
    BISAC: RELIGION / Christian Living / Prayer | FAMILY & RELATIONSHIPS / Parenting / General
Classification: LCC BV4529 .B3555 2022 | DDC 248.3/2--dc23
LC record available at https://lccn.loc.gov/2021045636

Printed in the United States of America
23 24 25 26 27 28 29 30 / 9 8 7 6 5 4 3 2

I have no greater joy than to hear that
my children are walking in the truth.

3 JOHN 4

To my children, with faith, hope, and love.

Contents

Acknowledgments   11

Introduction   13

Week 1: Don't Cry (Luke 7:13)   **15**

Day 1   Eternal Encouragement (2 Thessalonians 2:16–17)   18
Day 2   When You Feel Like a Failure as a Parent (Jude 24)   20
Day 3   David, Goliath, and the Name of the Lord (1 Samuel 17:45) 22
Day 4   Casting Cares (1 Peter 5:7)   24
Day 5   A Place for Anger (in God's Hands) (James 1:19–20)   26
Day 6   On Your Shoulders (Psalm 140:7)   28
Day 7   In the Shadow of Your Wing (Psalm 63:7)   30

Week 2: The Power of a Parent's Prayers (Mark 10:13–14)   **32**

Day 8   When You Can't Change the Consequences of
         His Actions (2 Samuel 19:4)   34
Day 9   The Son of These Tears (Job 16:19–20)   36
Day 10   Bring the Boy to Me (Mark 9:19)   38
Day 11   The Plans You Have (Jeremiah 29:11)   40
Day 12   Restored (Job 33:26)   42
Day 13   The Difference Prayer Makes (James 5:16)   44
Day 14   If I Should Die before She Wakes (I Pray the Lord Her Soul to Take)
         (Hebrews 11:13)   46

Week 3: Wanting What God Wants (Matthew 20:20)   **48**

Day 15   Open Doors (Daniel 1:9)   51
Day 16   The Way Out (1 Corinthians 10:13)   53
Day 17   For Open Eyes (Ephesians 1:18–19)   55
Day 18   Father, Forgive (Luke 23:33–34)   57
Day 19   God of the Second Chance (John 21:15)   59
Day 20   New Mercy! (Lamentations 3:22–23)   61
Day 21   Take Heart! (John 16:33)   63

Week 4: The Running Father (Luke 15:20)   65

Day 22   No Record of Wrongs (1 Corinthians 13:4–5)   68

Day 23   For Perfect Love to Drive Out Fear (1 John 4:18)   70

Day 24   Extra Miles (Matthew 5:41)   72

Day 25   For Grace to Abound at Home (2 Corinthians 9:8)   74

Day 26   You Promised! (Genesis 32:12)   76

Day 27   Thank You (Psalm 127:3)   78

Day 28   Blessed without Knowing It (Genesis 28:16)   80

Week 5: The Stretcher of Faith (Mark 2:5)   82

Day 29   Snatched from the Fire (Jude 22–23)   85

Day 30   A Softer Heart (Ezekiel 36:26–27)   87

Day 31   Whoever (John 3:16)   89

Day 32   A Better Attitude (Ephesians 4:22–24)   91

Day 33   Friends, and a Friend (Proverbs 18:24)   93

Day 34   Innocence Found (Isaiah 1:18)   95

Day 35   Praise Because You've Been There (Luke 19:41–42)   97

Week 6: Just Say the Word (Matthew 8:5–13)   99

Day 36   For Chains to Fall (Psalm 107:14)   102

Day 37   For an Honest Answer (Proverbs 24:26)   104

Day 38   Off Broadway (Matthew 7:13–14)   106

Day 39   Taming the Tongue (James 3:7–8)   108

Day 40   Run! (1 Corinthians 6:18–20)   110

Day 41   For Freedom from Substance Abuse (Luke 21:34)   112

Day 42   Praise for Small Victories (Zechariah 4:10)   114

Week 7: Coming to Our Senses (Luke 15:17)   116

Day 43   When You've Said Something You Regret (Psalm 141:3) 119

Day 44   Manipulated (Genesis 50:20)   121

Day 45   Songs in the Night (Psalm 42:8)   123

Day 46   Accepting Rejection (Isaiah 53:3)   125

Day 47   When Distance Separates (Isaiah 59:1)   127

Day 48   Praise in the Dark (Acts 16:25)   129

Day 49   Constant Help (Psalm 46:1)   131

Week 8: Treasured in Our Hearts (Luke 2:51)   **133**

Day 50   When She Hasn't Come Home Yet (Psalm 102:6–7)   136

Day 51   Light His Feet (Psalm 119:105)   138

Day 52   Shame Off Her! (Romans 10:11)   140

Day 53   What the Locusts Have Eaten (Joel 2:25)   142

Day 54   Straight Steps (Proverbs 3:5–6)   144

Day 55   Of God's Choosing (Genesis 24:42)   146

Day 56   Inexhaustible (Isaiah 40:30–31)   148

Week 9: Waiting for an Answer (Matthew 15:23)   **150**

Day 57   A Discerning Heart (Daniel 12:3)   153

Day 58   Wonderful Light (1 Peter 2:9)   155

Day 59   Back to Flame (Isaiah 42:3)   157

Day 60   Dressed in Armor (Ephesians 6:11)   159

Day 61   When Angels Sing (Luke 15:10)   161

Day 62   For the Keeping of Angels (Matthew 18:10)   163

Day 63   Quiet in His Love (Zephaniah 3:17)   165

Week 10: Who Sinned? (John 9:2)   **167**

Day 64   Sins of the Parents? (John 9:1–2)   170

Day 65   Strength to Go On (Habakkuk 3:17–19)   172

Day 66   How Long, O Lord? (Psalm 6:3)   174

Day 67   When You're "Prayed Out" (Romans 8:34)   176

Day 68   When He Is Older (Proverbs 22:6)   178

Day 69   When Sorrow and Sighing Flee Away (Isaiah 35:10)   180

Day 70   More Than I Ask or Imagine (Ephesians 3:20–21)   182

Week 11: The Good Shepherd (Luke 15:2–7)   **184**

Day 71   Your Dream for My Child (Joel 2:28)   187

Day 72   Turning Hearts (Malachi 4:6)   189

Day 73   The Contender (Isaiah 49:25)   191

Day 74   Running to Jesus (Proverbs 18:10)   193

Day 75   Inner Beauty (1 Peter 3:3–4)   195

Day 76   Every Blessing (James 1:17)   197

Day 77   Through All Generations (Psalm 119:90)   199

Week 12: Everything Is Possible (Mark 9:20–24)   **201**

Day 78   A Larger Lion (1 Peter 5:8)   204

Day 79   Long in the Land (Ephesians 6:1–3)   206

Day 80   Sitting in the Courtroom (Psalm 130:3–4)   208

Day 81   Should Have, Would Have, Could Have (Isaiah 48:18)   210

Day 82   Everything She Ever Wanted (Isaiah 32:17)   212

Day 83   In All Things, God (Romans 8:28)   214

Day 84   River of Delights (Psalm 36:7–8)   216

Week 13: God's Timing (Mark 5:36)   **218**

Day 85   Those Who Are with Us (2 Kings 6:16–17)   221

Day 86   For Strength to Love (Romans 8:35)   223

Day 87   Hiding Place (Psalm 32:7)   225

Day 88   Always There (Matthew 28:20)   227

Day 89   He Is Yours, and So Am I (Luke 1:38)   229

Day 90   I Believe (2 Corinthians 5:7)   231

Conclusion   233

For Group Discussion and Prayer   235

Resources for Those Who Love Prodigals   249

Sources   251

Index   253

About the Author   255

Acknowledgments

God gives us people along the way who help make writing books easier and also help with the challenges of parenting prodigals. I've needed *both*, and I'm deeply thankful for all of them.

Annette Gysen, Judith Markham, Carol Holquist, Ken Petersen, and Katy Pent, your vision for this book has been such a blessing! Miranda Gardner and Dawn Anderson, your careful editing and heart for God's Word are an answer to prayer! What a joy it is to work with you!

I'm especially thankful for the praying people of Peace Church in Durham, North Carolina: Ken and Barbara Davis, Bob and Marty Griffin, Bob and Pam Dodson, Bruce and Jan Gray, Lynn Wiemann, and Betsy Hamilton (and many others!). You have shown me the Savior again and again. Daniel and Jenn Summers, Elizabeth Mixon, Mark Allen, and Mike Ashcraft from Port City Church, God has used your kindness to our son to work miracles, and we praise Him for you!

Don Westbrook, Dub Karriker, Dick Bigelow, Mac Bayer, Scott McClintock, your faithfulness in prayer is changing our city, and it has given me strength and comfort time and again.

Dave Wineman, Keith Cobb, Frank Carter, David Beaty, Howard and Margaret Shockley, and Dick and Shirilee Little, your wisdom and compassion in challenging seasons have been a gift from God. Bob Mayer, Joel Collier, Garth Roselle, John Holecek, your encouragement has helped keep me going! Sister Damian and Sister Cam and Kathy from the Avila Center in Durham, you opened a "Bethany" place of rest for me for writing and praying. May God bless you for it!

Cari, you're not only my beautiful wife of thirty-five years but you're also the most amazing mother I've ever seen. This book would not have happened without you.

All praise belongs to the one true God, my Savior—Father, Son, and Holy Spirit—who gives life and breath and every hope and blessing. Soli Deo gloria!

Introduction

*Prodigals are not limited in gender, race, age or color. They do have
one thing in common: They have left home, and they are missed.*

—RUTH BELL GRAHAM

When you have a prodigal child, prayer doesn't always come easily. You
know you *need* to pray, but you don't know where to begin. That's why this
book was written.

God blessed me with two prodigals. I use the word *blessed* because
they are a gift, just like every child. Prodigals are an especially precious gift
because they teach us much, including patience, the depth of our own need
for forgiveness, and continual dependence on God in prayer. When our
children bring us to our knees, we're in the best position for God to help us.

Some of God's best lessons are His most challenging. When we come
to the end of our own strength, we learn to rely on His. Through prayer
He takes us by the hand and leads us to fresh places of grace that we never
would have seen if the challenges had not come.

Prayers for Prodigals will help you pray, and it will remind you of the
power of God to answer prayer for your prodigal child. Ninety Scripture-
based prayers, one for each day of the week, cover many of the emotional
and practical challenges faced by the parents of prodigals. Each week
begins with a brief meditation that includes personal stories or examples
of how God has moved in the lives of prodigals in the past, and most
importantly, inspiration from the life and promises of Jesus. Some of the
prayers are written for a son and some for a daughter, but they will work
for either if you change the pronouns as you pray.

I hope you will use the prayers as a starting point for your own prayers.
That's why an "amen" hasn't been added to most of them. I hope you'll add
thoughts of your own. Bring the specific needs of your child before God
and keep praying in Jesus's name for your child's salvation.

Besides praying on your own, I suggest gathering others to pray with you as well. A husband and wife praying for their child make a powerful team. Some parents choose a particular hour of the night to pray for their child, and they let their child know that they are praying at that time. Some choose a day to fast together or ask others to intercede daily with them for specific needs in their child's life. Praying for a son or daughter at a prayer meeting as Jim Cymbala did (see Week 5, "The Stretcher of Faith") can open the door for God to move in your child's life in a beautiful way.

You'll find further encouragement for prayer at my website at JamesBanks.org, where we have a "Prodigal Prayer Wall" for sharing requests and answers to prayer. If you have a story of how God has moved in your prodigal's life in answer to praying through this book, I would love to hear about it! If you would like to know more about what God has done in one of my prodigal's lives in answer to prayer since this book was first written, you may be interested in reading *Hope Lies Ahead,* which I cowrote with my son, Geoffrey.

This latest edition of *Prayers for Prodigals* offers several improvements, including additional prayer helps, discussion questions for groups, and helpful reading resources. It is my heartfelt prayer that God will use this book to change your child's eternal future, and through *your* prayers bring your son or daughter into a vital relationship with Jesus. Nothing in this world or the next could possibly matter more.

Don't Cry

*When the Lord saw her, his heart went out
to her and he said, "Don't cry."*

LUKE 7:13

Ruth and Billy Graham knew well the struggles of parenting a prodigal. In her book *Prodigals and Those Who Love Them,* Ruth tells of waking up worried in the middle of the night:

> It was early in the morning in another country. Exhausted as I was, I awoke around three o'clock. The name of someone I loved dearly flashed into my mind. It was like an electric shock.
>
> Instantly I was wide awake. I knew there would be no more sleep for me for the rest of the night. So I lay there and prayed for the one who was trying hard to run from God. When it is dark and the imagination runs wild, there are fears only a mother can understand.
>
> Suddenly the Lord said to me, "Quit studying the problems and start studying the promises."
>
> Now, God has never spoken to me audibly, but there is no mistaking when He speaks. So I turned on the light, got out my Bible, and the first verses that came to me were Philippians 4:6–7: "Be careful for nothing; but in every thing by prayer and supplication *with thanksgiving* let your requests be made known unto God. And the peace of God, which passeth all understanding,

shall keep your hearts and minds through Christ Jesus" (italics mine). . . . Suddenly I realized the missing ingredient in my prayers had been "with thanksgiving." So I put down my Bible and spent time worshiping Him for who and what He is. This covers more territory than any mortal can comprehend. Even contemplating what little we do know dissolves doubts, reinforces faith, and restores joy.[1]

Sometimes we have to purposefully choose Jesus when it may be the last thing we "feel" like doing. Peace and confidence come when we drop our distractions and focus on Jesus alone, because "he himself is our peace" (Ephesians 2:14). When nerves are raw, emotions tense, and schedules overwhelming, we *need* to go to our rooms, "close the door and pray" (Matthew 6:6). We have to drop everything and spend time with God, remembering that He is "majestic in holiness, awesome in glory, working wonders" (Exodus 15:11). As we do, He will meet us in our place of need.

The New Testament tells us that Jesus was entering the gates of "a town called Nain" when he encountered a large funeral procession for the only son of a widow. Luke carefully points out that "when the Lord saw her, his heart went out to her and he said, 'Don't cry.'" Then Jesus reached out, touched the coffin, and *stopped* the procession. He spoke to the young man and raised him from the dead. Then Jesus "gave him back to his mother" (Luke 7:11–15).

The word Luke uses to describe Jesus's heart going out to the mother implies a depth of compassion from the center of His being (literally, His "gut"). When we weep over our own children, we can rest assured our Savior's heart goes out to us in the same way. He longs to comfort us and help us as He alone can.

But for that to happen, sometimes we have to wait for Jesus. We have to allow Him to *stop* us in what we're doing. Then we need to place what we're facing in His hands. The woman had no idea what Jesus was about to do. What He did defied logic and changed *everything*.

---

1. Graham, *Prodigals and Those Who Love Them*, 50–51.

The funeral procession became a party. Luke writes, "They were all filled with awe and praised God" (7:16). Weeping turned into worship, and despair into delight. All because of Jesus. He had brought them unexpected joy.

Before Jesus stopped the procession that day, they had no idea who He was. But *we* do. We already know Him as "the Messiah, the Son of the living God," always worthy of worship (Matthew 16:16). He is "the resurrection and the life" (John 11:25), who will give life to our kids.

Knowing that, we can stop putting one foot in front of the other and wait for him.

He is coming our way.

And He has something to say to our sons and our daughters.

Come, ye sinners, poor and needy,
weak and wounded, sick and sore;
Jesus ready stands to save you,
full of pity, love and power.

—JOSEPH HART,

"COME, YE SINNERS, POOR AND NEEDY"

Eternal Encouragement

May our Lord Jesus Christ himself and God our Father,
who loved us and by his grace gave us eternal encouragement
and good hope, encourage your hearts
and strengthen you in every good deed and word.

2 THESSALONIANS 2:16–17

"Eternal encouragement."
I *love* those words, Father.
"Eternal encouragement *and* good hope."
I really need both right now.
Not just for me, but for my child.
He is far from you and needs to come home,
    and he needs me to pray.
He needs me to pray now more than ever before,
    and you alone can help me to do that.
Help me to pray, Lord Jesus. I ask you to *teach* me to pray,
    like you did for the disciples (Luke 11:1).
Help me to pray every day, throughout the day.
Fill me with your Spirit and let your love flow through me into my
    child's life.
Like the widow who "kept coming" to the judge's door
    until her request was answered (Luke 18:3),
        help me to persevere in praying "day and night" (Luke 18:7)
        so that I will see real progress in my child's heart.

Jesus, you said that "everything is possible for one
who believes" (Mark 9:23).
"I do believe; help me overcome my unbelief!" (Mark 9:24).
Save my son, Lord! I thank you in advance for what you will do to
rescue him from "the dominion of darkness" and bring him into
your "kingdom of light" and love (Colossians 1:12–13).
I believe that you will do this because "we live by faith,
not by sight" (2 Corinthians 5:7).
I believe that you will do this because you have promised it.
Your Word says that "from everlasting to everlasting the Lord's
love is with those who fear him, and his righteousness with
their children's children" (Psalm 103:17).
Thank you for the eternal encouragement you alone can give.
I am encouraged! You are God, and you answer prayer!
Your "love never fails" (1 Corinthians 13:8).
You have brought my own prodigal heart home,
and I thank you that you will do the same for my child.
"I love you, Lord, my strength" (Psalm 18:1), and I praise you for
the day when my child will love you too!

———

**How has God been faithful to you in encouraging ways in the past?
Take a moment to praise Him for this.**

DAY 2

When You Feel Like a Failure as a Parent

To him who is able to keep you from stumbling and to present you
before his glorious presence without fault and with great joy . . .

JUDE 24

I don't know how many times I've felt like there must have been something
more I could have done as a parent, Father.
If I had just had more of your love, strength, and wisdom, perhaps
my child would have made choices that would have kept her
close to you.
I would have changed some things if I had known then
what I know now.
Forgive me, Father, where I "have sinned" and
fallen "short of" your best (Romans 3:23).
Because I can't change what has already happened,
I pray that you will open my heart to new things you are doing,
so that I "do not dwell on the past" (Isaiah 43:18).
Help me instead to "press on toward the goal to win the prize for which
God has called me heavenward in Christ Jesus" (Philippians 3:14).
You've told me that "my grace is sufficient for you,
for my power is made perfect in weakness" (2 Corinthians 12:9).
Thank you for reminding me that I must depend on you, Father,
and that you are able to present me before you
"without fault and with great joy."

Help me to be "very careful" how I live,
"not as unwise, but as wise."
Help me to make "the most of every opportunity" to point my daughter
to you with consistency and sincerity (Ephesians 5:15–16).
Because you show "favor to the humble" (Proverbs 3:34),
help me to set an example in everything I do,
just as you have done for me (John 13:15).
Help me to keep my eyes "fixed on you, Sovereign LORD" (Psalm 141:8)
so that I will not rely on myself or my own strength
but be strong in you, in your "mighty power" (Ephesians 6:10).
Where I have my blind sides, Father, "forgive my hidden faults"
(Psalm 19:12).
Let nothing about me be a "stumbling block" (Romans 14:13).
Help me to let my "light shine" before my daughter, Lord, so that
she may see the good I do and praise you for it (Matthew 5:16).
Direct my heart into your "love and Christ's perseverance"
(2 Thessalonians 3:5).
Holy Spirit, let me "be filled with" you (Ephesians 5:18)
so that "rivers of living water will flow from within" me (John 7:38),
"welling up to eternal life" (John 4:14).
Not just for me, but for the child I love.

———

Scripture shows us several parents who were devoted to God—among them
Samuel, David, and Jehoshaphat—who also had children who went astray.
Talk this over with God, and ask Him for the difference He alone can make
in your prodigal's heart and life.

David, Goliath, and the Name of the Lord

*David said to the Philistine, "You come against me
with sword and spear and javelin, but I come against
you in the name of the LORD Almighty,
the God of the armies of Israel, whom you have defied."*

1 SAMUEL 17:45

Sometimes encountering the rebellion in my child's life
    feels like I'm facing a giant, Lord.
We're up against so much that it's hard to know where to begin.
So instead of sizing up the giant, I'd rather keep my eyes on you.
You are the commander of "the armies of heaven" (Revelation 19:14).
Nothing can stand against you!
Like David when he faced Goliath, it is "in the name of the LORD
    Almighty" that I take my stand.
Only your power can win this battle, because "our struggle is not against
    flesh and blood, but against the rulers, against the authorities, against
    the powers of this dark world and against the spiritual forces of evil
    in the heavenly realms" (Ephesians 6:12).
The struggle is not with my child, but with the spiritual forces
    that influence him to turn away from you.
I come against the giant of rebellion in my child's life in the name
    of "the LORD strong and mighty, the LORD mighty in battle"
    (Psalm 24:8).

Because you are the LORD "who is striking the blow" (Ezekiel 7:9 NLT),

I pray that you will use every means to cause the giant to fall.

This isn't about my will in his life. It's about yours.

I ask that you, "the Holy One" who has no equal (Isaiah 40:25),

will come between my child and anything that could cause him harm.

I pray that "through the unfailing love of the Most High he will not be

shaken," but only drawn closer to you (Psalm 21:7).

Then he will know you as "the LORD Our Righteous Savior" (Jeremiah 33:16).

Because you are "the LORD, who heals" (Exodus 15:26),

I pray you will restore his relationship with you in every way,

that he may be eternally blessed.

Thank you that "it is not by strength that one prevails" (1 Samuel 2:9),

but only through your grace and awesome power to answer prayer!

I praise you, Father, that the giant of rebellion is very small compared to you.

It is in the invincible name of the Father, and the Son, and the Holy Spirit

that I lift this prayer with love to you.

———

What "giants" have you seen God conquer in your life or the lives of others? Ask Him to do it again against any giants you face in your prodigal's life.

DAY 4

Casting Cares

Cast all your anxiety on him because he cares for you.

1 PETER 5:7

How do you do it, Lord?

You're able to take all of the cares of the world on your shoulders,
   including my cares for my child.

You're able to carry them continually!

Not only do you carry them but you're also able do something about them.

How amazing you are! Thank you for caring for me and my child.

"Power belongs to you, God," and "with you, Lord, is unfailing love"
   (Psalm 62:11–12).

I come to you today to cast all my cares on you.

More than anything else, I ask that my daughter will come to know you,
   Lord Jesus (Ephesians 1:17).

I long for her to have a living relationship with you.

   If she walked with you, how blessed she would be!

I cast this care and ask that your Spirit draw her to you.

I pray she will repent and turn to you and prove her repentance
   by the things she does (Acts 26:20).

I'm also concerned for her safety, Lord. The choices she's made and the
   friends she's chosen have frequently put her in harm's way.

I know only part of it. But you know all of it.

Only you can keep her safe, Lord, though I try too.

Your "forces are beyond number,"
   and those under your command are "mighty" (Joel 2:11).

Please send your angels to watch over her.

May your "power and might" protect her, Lord (Jeremiah 16:21).

I cast this care and place her in your arms again.

There's no better place for her to be.

I also lift her future to you, Father.

I pray she will seek your kingdom with her heart, mind, and strength and work for what pleases you.

I pray that you will be in her and she in you (John 17:23) so that she will have the joy of knowing you "face to face" (1 Corinthians 13:12).

Until that day, I pray that your "divine power" will give her everything she needs "for living a godly life" (2 Peter 1:3 NLT).

You have given us such "very great and precious promises," Lord (2 Peter 1:4).

I praise you that the weight of my cares, no matter how heavy they may seem to me, are light to you and easy for you to carry.

"Praise be to the Lord, to God our Savior, who daily bears our burdens" (Psalm 68:19).

I cast *all* my cares upon you!

———

As you pray, imagine that you are holding your cares in your hands. Hold your hands up to God and ask Him to take every one of them.

A Place for Anger
(in God's Hands)

My dear brothers and sisters, take note of this: Everyone should be
quick to listen, slow to speak and slow to become angry, because
human anger does not produce the righteousness that God desires.

JAMES 1:19-20

Father, one of the harder challenges I face with my child is what to do
when I am angry.

I want to be careful not to discipline him while unrighteously angry,
because that will give him cause to resent what I've done and rebel all
the more.

Your Word tells me, "do not embitter your children, or
they will become discouraged" (Colossians 3:21).

Today I ask that you will help me to be "slow to speak
and slow to become angry" (James 1:19).

Give me grace to "follow the way of love" (1 Corinthians 14:1).

With that as my aim, I'm going to practice counting to ten and placing
my anger in your hands.

One. I acknowledge that "human anger does not produce the
righteousness" that you desire, especially when it comes to
my son's life. Show me your way, Lord.

Two. Let me follow your wisdom and not sin (Psalm 4:4) when I cannot
avoid being angry.

Three. Help me to search my heart and "be silent" (Psalm 4:4), waiting for your Spirit to lead me, because "the mind governed by the Spirit is life and peace" (Romans 8:6).

Four. Make me "quick to listen" (James 1:19). Help me to respond and not react, so I will not jump to conclusions or make hasty decisions that I will regret later.

Five. Help me to keep my head "in all situations" (2 Timothy 4:5), so that I may have wisdom to direct my son in the way he should go.

Six. When the time comes to discipline my son, fill me with an extra measure of love for him, because "the one who loves" his son "is careful to discipline" him (Proverbs 13:24).

Seven. Give me grace to be careful with my words, so that even when I am angry I will say "only what is helpful for building others up according to their needs, that it may benefit those who listen" (Ephesians 4:29).

Eight. Once I have disciplined my son, help me to "restore him gently" (Galatians 6:1) and to remind him of how much we both love him.

Nine. Help me to "not let the sun go down" while I am angry (Ephesians 4:26), so that I will not harbor any resentment in my heart for anything he has done.

Ten. Please give me grace to "pray continually" (1 Thessalonians 5:17), so that I may place my son and myself in your hands moment by moment.

Then together we will walk from a season of anger into a season of your blessing and joy.

———

Where have you faced anger about your prodigal's situation?
Talk openly with God about this, and thank Him that no situation is
too difficult for Him to handle.

DAY 6

On Your Shoulders

Sovereign Lord, my strong deliverer . . .

PSALM 140:7

I remember when he was little and he loved to have me
    carry him on my shoulders.
He felt bigger there—taller, stronger, able to face anything.
He felt safe and secure.
I can't carry him anymore, Lord. Not like that.
But I'm reminded of your Word: "The one the Lord loves
    rests between his shoulders" (Deuteronomy 33:12).
Father, I ask that you pick him up and carry him.
You are our "strong deliverer" (Psalm 140:7).
I praise you that we face no situation that is greater than you.
I'm reminded of what Moses told Israel: "You saw how the Lord your God
    carried you, as a father carries his son" (Deuteronomy 1:31).
Father, my son needs you to carry him now.
I pray he will recognize his own limitations and understand his need
    for you.
Help him to humble himself before you,
    so that you will lift him up (James 4:10).
Give him grace to understand how your
    "power is made perfect in weakness" (2 Corinthians 12:9).
Let him hear you say, "Even to your old age and gray hairs I am he,
    I am he who will sustain you. I have made you
    and I will carry you" (Isaiah 46:4).

You have carried me, Father, again and again.
I praise you for all the times you've given me hope,
    just what I needed at just the right moment.
Because "power belongs to you, God" and "with you, Lord, is unfailing
    love" (Psalm 62:11–12), I thank you that you will move in my son's life
    in answer to this prayer.
I pray my son will long to spend time with you
    and know the comfort you give to those who love you.
I look forward to the day he will say, "My soul finds rest in God;
    my salvation comes from him" (Psalm 62:1).
Just as you told your people in the wilderness, "I carried you on
    eagles' wings and brought you to myself" (Exodus 19:4),
    bring him out of the wilderness that he's in
    and let him "see your face" (Psalm 17:15).
I look forward to the day that you will "[lift] up" his head (Psalm 3:3 CSB).
And on that wonderful day he will see all the way from here
    to eternity!

————

Imagine as you pray that you are holding your prodigal in your arms.
Now extend your arms, and lift him or her to the Lord, asking for His help.

In the Shadow of Your Wing

Because you are my help, I sing in the shadow of your wings.

PSALM 63:7

How good it is just to take a moment with you, Lord!

Thank you for your faithfulness to me and my child.

Just like Jacob, "I am unworthy of all the kindness and faithfulness
    you have shown," Father (Genesis 32:10).

You are always there, the one who watches over us (Psalm 121:5).

You have been so good to us! How can I not praise you?

"I will praise you, Lord my God, with all of my heart" (Psalm 86:12).

"I will praise the LORD, who counsels me" (Psalm 16:7).

"I will praise you as long as I live" (Psalm 63:4).

"I will praise you more and more" (Psalm 71:14).

Thank you that you can even give me grace to praise you in difficult places.

When challenges come, I "take refuge
    in the shadow of your wings" (Psalm 36:7).

When you give and when you take away,
    "may the name of the LORD be praised" (Job 1:21).

"Why should I fear when evil days come . . . ?" (Psalm 49:5)

You are "the faithful God" (Deuteronomy 7:9).

Help me to offer "a sacrifice of praise" to you (Hebrews 13:15).

There's no better place than the "shadow of your wings,"
    and no better love than your "faithful love" (Isaiah 55:3).

No matter how difficult the day,
    I praise you that it will not last,

because "you guide me with your counsel,

and afterward you will take me into glory" (Psalm 73:24).

I pray for the grace to praise you every day, because you always deserve it.

Help me to say with David, "I will extol the LORD at all times;

his praise will always be on my lips" (Psalm 34:1).

You give "peace at all times and in every way" (2 Thessalonians 3:16).

You are "my strength" (Exodus 15:2), "my joy and my delight" (Psalm 43:4),

"my Lord and my God" (John 20:28).

"Sovereign LORD, my strong deliverer" (Psalm 140:7), because your mercy

extends "from generation to generation" (Luke 1:50),

I ask that my daughter will one day know your love

and take refuge in you as well.

Then "I will praise you forever," my Savior, "for what you have done"

(Psalm 52:9 NLT).

Better still, together "we will praise your name forever" (Psalm 44:8).

———

As you place your head on your pillow tonight, imagine that you are leaning on Jesus (think of John, leaning on Jesus in John 13:23), and rest in His loving care for you.

The Power of a Parent's Prayers

People were bringing little children to Jesus for him to place his hands on them, but the disciples rebuked them. When Jesus saw this, he was indignant. He said to them, "Let the little children come to me, and do not hinder them, for the kingdom of God belongs to such as these."

MARK 10:13–14

When you're the parent of a prodigal child, you're sometimes the recipient of unsolicited advice. When our daughter ran away at the age of fifteen, one well-meaning professional advised us to "let her fall flat on her face."

"After all," he continued, "kids have to learn from their own mistakes."

Some of that advice is sound. There are lessons our children have to learn for themselves that we cannot teach them, try as we may. But the day we found our daughter and brought her home (against her will), she had been befriended by another teenage runaway with an adult boyfriend fresh out of jail. They were encouraging her to leave the state with them. Letting her "fall flat on her face" would have been a dangerous thing to do.

It may be difficult for other parents to understand *exactly* what you're up against with a prodigal son or daughter, especially if they haven't walked the same road with their own children. But God understands. He knows what it's like to have a world full of prodigals. And he waits for us to bring *ours* to Him through committed, passionate prayer.

Prayer combined with a believing mother's or father's love is powerful. When placed in Jesus's hands, it is invincible. Obstacles may come when you least expect them, but perseverance in prayer will lead to a breakthrough. Our God is the "One who breaks open the way" (Micah 2:13). Jesus was *indignant* with the disciples for creating an obstacle when they rebuked parents for bringing their children to Him for His blessing. "Let the little children come to me," he said (Mark 10:13–14). *Indignant* is used nowhere else in the New Testament to describe how Jesus felt about something, and it sets apart His passion for our children and how much He wants to bless them.

We must do whatever it takes to bring our prodigals to Jesus in prayer, because Jesus wants to bless us and our children through our prayers. The world's perspective is that a "blessed" child is one who grows up to be happy, well-adjusted, and successful in a career. But even "successful" kids can be prodigals, and Christian parents who have them have to be careful not to be lulled into a false sense of security. God has given us our children for eternal purposes, and there is no greater blessing and inheritance we can pass on to them than our prayers for their salvation.

Most importantly, we are blessed to have a Savior who longs for our children to come to Him! Let others say what they will. We have *His* promises, and that is all that matters. Remember what the Pharisees and teachers of the law muttered about *Jesus*? "This man welcomes sinners and eats with them" (Luke 15:2).

There's a place in His heart for prodigals. Especially *our* prodigals as we bring them before Him in prayer.

> *My mother's prayers! Oh, my sweet, blessed mother's prayers.*
> *Did ever a boy have such a mother as I had?*
> *For twenty-five years I have not heard her pray, till*
> *tonight. I have heard all her prayers over again.*

—TESTIMONY OF A MAN WHO CAME TO CHRIST DURING THE 1857–59
PRAYER MEETING REVIVAL, YEARS AFTER HIS MOTHER'S DEATH

When You Can't Change the Consequences of His Actions

The king covered his face and cried aloud,
"O my son Absalom! O Absalom, my son, my son!"

2 SAMUEL 19:4

I remember when my son was little, Father,
 and his problems were so much easier to fix.
A skinned knee, a lost toy, a flat tire on his bike—those were things
 I could more or less handle.
That has changed now.
He faces problems that I would love to make go away,
 but it's no longer in my power to do that.
Now he has to face the consequences of his actions,
 and it isn't easy, for him or for me.
I can't imagine how David felt when he faced his son's rebellion,
 but David's words stay with me: "Be gentle with the young man . . .
 for my sake" (2 Samuel 18:5).
I ask for my son what David asked for his, Father:
 Please "be gentle with the young man."
I thank you that I don't ask this of mere human beings, as David did.
I ask it of the One who "has compassion on all he has made"
 (Psalm 145:9).
You are "rich in mercy" (Ephesians 2:4),
 and I'm grateful for the mercy you have for my son, Lord.

I understand that if he does not face the consequences of his actions,
he may not learn from them.

But I would rather have him fall into your hands, for your
"mercy is great," than "into human hands" (2 Samuel 24:14).

That is why I place his circumstances into your hands,
and ask that you bless him as you alone can.

You have told me, "as the heavens are higher than the earth,
so are my ways higher than your ways
and my thoughts than your thoughts" (Isaiah 55:9).

You see the best way through his problems, Father!

I pray you will bring good from them
that could not have come about any other way.

I love you, Lord, and praise you that "in all things" you are at work
"for the good of those who love" you (Romans 8:28).

I pray that my son will love you too!

Use *all of this* to turn his heart to you, because that is what matters most.

I pray that he will come to you to "have life, and have it
to the full" (John 10:10).

If he has that, he has all he will ever need.

————

As you pray for your prodigal, humble yourself before God. Think of ways
God has been merciful to you despite your actions or choices, and praise
Him for His kindness to you.

The Son of These Tears

Even now my witness is in heaven; my advocate is on high.
My intercessor is my friend as my eyes pour out tears to God.

JOB 16:19-20

"It is not possible that the son of these tears should perish."[2]

Those words spoken to a mother centuries ago as she prayed for her son
encourage me too, Lord.

Not only did you save her son, Augustine,[3]
but you used him to bring many others to you!

Lord Jesus, I thank you that I am not the only one praying for my son.

I praise you that you are "interceding for us" in
heaven (Romans 8:34).

How blessed I am that "my intercessor is my friend" (Job 16:20).

Even my tears matter to you. You keep track of every one—
"are they not in your record?" (Psalm 56:8).

Thank you, Father, that there is hope for "the son of these tears."

You promise in your Word that "those who sow with tears will reap
with songs of joy" (Psalm 126:5).

Thank you that I may reap a harvest in my son's life as I pray for him!

Lord Jesus, just as you "offered up prayers and petitions with fervent cries
and tears" and were heard because of your "reverent submission"

---

2. Augustine, *Confessions*, 3.12, available at ccel.org/ccel/augustine/confess.iv.xii.html.

3. God would use Augustine's faith to inspire generations to believe in Jesus. He became the most influential theologian in the early centuries of the church, and his influence is still felt today. For more about Augustine's early life, see Week 13, "God's Timing."

(Hebrews 5:7), help me to pray with passion and commitment, and to "pray continually" (1 Thessalonians 5:17).

I believe one reason you've given my son to me is so I can pray for him to have the joy of knowing you forever.

Praying for him is one of the greatest purposes of my life, and I don't want to miss it. Most of all, I don't want *him* to miss *you*!

Help him understand that you are "gracious and compassionate," and that you will not turn your face from him if he returns to you (2 Chronicles 30:9).

I pray he will know the riches of your "kindness, restraint and patience" (Romans 2:4 CSB), and be filled "with your unfailing love" (Psalm 90:14).

Your "love endures forever" (1 Chronicles 16:34). We will not have enough time, even with eternal life, to give you all the love you deserve.

I praise you for the day you will "wipe away the tears from all faces" (Isaiah 25:8), even from the face of "the son of these tears"!

Then we will "weep no more" because you will be our joy (Isaiah 30:19), and we will worship you, "King of the ages" (Revelation 15:3 RSV), through every age to come!

Rest before the Lord, and imagine Him wiping every tear from your eyes, and from your prodigal's as well!

Bring the Boy to Me

"You unbelieving generation," Jesus replied, "how long shall I stay with you? How long shall I put up with you? Bring the boy to me."

MARK 9:19

Here he is, Lord.

This is my son, and he needs you desperately.

I bring him to you, all that he is and all that is going on in his life.

His life is beyond my power to repair or set right.

I ask you to touch him and help him, Lord!

Years ago when you told the disciples, "Bring the boy to me,"
　　you began the greatest blessing of the child's life.

Darkness had to flee. It could not stand in your presence.

　　So I bring my son into "the light of your presence"
　　again today (Psalm 89:15).

I'm reminded of what you told your disciples.

　　The child could be set free "only by prayer" (Mark 9:29).

The disciples had tried everything they could think of,
　　but no matter how hard they tried in their own strength,
　　"they could not" make any difference (Mark 9:18).

You rebuked them for their lack of faith. Then you said,
　　"Everything is possible for one who believes" (Mark 9:23).

I'm beginning to understand how much I need to bring my son to you
　　in faithful, believing prayer.

He needs the difference only you can make for him.

How wonderful that father must have felt when he walked away
with his son, happy and healthy and standing strong.
He had brought his son to you, and you freed the boy!
Lord Jesus, I look forward to that day in my son's life as well,
the day he meets you and is transformed by your love,
rescued "from the dominion of darkness," and brought
"into the kingdom of the Son" (Colossians 1:13).
What a day that will be!
There will be "rejoicing in heaven" (Luke 15:7) and if I'm still here,
on earth as well!
By faith I see it coming, and I pray that day will come soon.
I believe you will save my son and that nothing will stand in
your way!
I look forward to that moment when "the day dawns and the morning
star rises" in his heart (2 Peter 1:19).
Please, Lord, could that day be today?

———————

**Praise God that He is able to do even more for your prodigal than you
can "ask or imagine" (Ephesians 3:20), and bring him or her before Him
again in prayer.**

The Plans You Have

"For I know the plans I have for you," declares the LORD, "plans to prosper you and not to harm you, plans to give you hope and a future."

JEREMIAH 29:11

I want your plans for my child, Lord, not mine.

My plans still have too much of the world in them: this school, that career path, that success . . .

Forgive me, Father, because too many times I have had in mind not "the concerns of God, but merely human concerns" (Mark 8:33).

I ask that you lift my eyes to a more lasting vision, Father.

Your plans for my child would take my breath away!

"How precious to me are your thoughts, God!" (Psalm 139:17).

Your thoughts are "too wonderful for me to know" (Job 42:3).

Your plan for my child is perfect,

and it magnificently exceeds the scope of my vision.

May "your will be done" in her life, Father (Matthew 6:10).

Today I ask for eternal things for my daughter.

I ask that she will be someone "after" your "own heart" (1 Samuel 13:14), who makes you her trust, "who does not look to the proud" (Psalm 40:4) or the ways of this world.

I pray that she "may live a life worthy of" you "and may please" you "in every way: bearing fruit in every good work, growing in the knowledge of" all that you are, "being strengthened with all power according to" your "glorious might" (Colossians 1:10–11).

Just as "all the days ordained for" her "were written in your book before one of them came to be" (Psalm 139:16), I pray that you will use even this season of rebellion in her life for eternal purposes.

Once she turns "from the error of" her way (James 5:20), I ask that she will "lead many to righteousness" (Daniel 12:3).

"You can do all things," Lord! "No purpose of yours can be thwarted" (Job 42:2).

Because "all things hold together" in you (Colossians 1:17), I ask that you hold her together when she seems to be falling apart.

Help her discover your plans and purposes for her life and love you for them!

I pray that you will prosper my daughter not only in this world, but especially in the world to come.

May you be her hope and her future (Jeremiah 29:11), because you "have the supremacy" in everything (Colossians 1:18).

———

Thank God that His plans for your prodigal are perfect, and ask Him to help you want what He wants for him or her.

DAY 12

Restored

He will pray to God, and God will delight in him. That person will see his face with a shout of joy, and God will restore his righteousness to him.

JOB 33:26 CSB

"He will pray to God, and God will delight in him. That person will see his
    face with a shout of joy, and God will restore his righteousness. . . ."
I can see my son in this verse! This is exactly what I want for him!
There is no joy like the joy you give. May he shout for joy to you!
There is nothing better than being restored to a right relationship with you.
I long to see my son wearing "a garment of praise instead of a spirit
    of despair."
I long to see him standing firm in you, an oak "of righteousness,
    a planting of the LORD for the display of his splendor" (Isaiah 61:3).
The oak may be in winter now, and much seems barren.
But spring will come! I pray he will turn his heart to you and
    "grow in the grace and knowledge" of all that you are (2 Peter 3:18).
You gave this child to me so I could raise him to believe in you.
You brought him from my body and placed him in my arms
    so I could pray for him to know you and love you for all eternity.
I have prayed for him, even before he was born,
    and now I will "not give up" praying for him (Galatians 6:9).
Today I "live by faith, not by sight" (2 Corinthians 5:7)
    as I wait for him to turn to you.
But "I remain confident of this: I will see the goodness of the LORD in the
    land of the living."

I will "be strong and take heart and wait for the LORD" (Psalm 27:13–14).
Seasons change! And this one will. The darkness will pass.
I stand on your truth: "The LORD is God,
   and he has made his light shine on us" (Psalm 118:27).
"Shine forth" (Psalm 80:1), Father!
Let your light overcome any darkness in his life!
"All things are possible" with you (Mark 10:27).
"Restore us, LORD God Almighty;
   make your face shine on us, that we may be saved" (Psalm 80:19).
By faith I see your face shining on my son,
   and him looking back at you, his face radiant with joy.
May "everlasting joy" be ours, Father (Isaiah 61:7). His, mine, and yours!
   To your glory, now and forever!

———

As you pray, imagine your prodigal as God desires him or her to be, standing strong as a new creation in Him (2 Corinthians 5:17).

The Difference Prayer Makes

The prayer of a righteous person is powerful and effective.

JAMES 5:16

Father, I praise you for the privilege of prayer.
You have answered my prayers so many times in so many ways!
Even when the answer wasn't what I was looking for at the time,
> you've shown me repeatedly that your "wisdom is profound" (Job 9:4).
Thank you that because of Jesus I may approach your "throne of grace with
> confidence," so that I may "receive mercy and find grace"
> in my "time of need" (Hebrews 4:16).
I have not earned the privilege of approaching the throne in prayer. I do
> not deserve it. You allow me to do so because of *your* goodness.
Your Word tells me that the prayers of a righteous man
> are powerful and effective—and this means that even *my* prayers are,
> because of what you have done for me.
Jesus has become for me my "righteousness, holiness and redemption"
> (1 Corinthians 1:30).
I can't thank you for that enough!
So I come to you again, Father, praising you that
> "Jesus came into the world to save sinners" (1 Timothy 1:15),
> and asking for your help for my daughter.
I praise you that my prayers can make a difference.
> You answer prayer! You choose to work through our prayers.
You promise to "give good gifts to those who ask" (Matthew 7:11).

Forgive me, Father, for my lack of faith,

and the times I've wondered if it really matters if I pray.

How could you not answer prayer?

You are "the compassionate and gracious God, slow to anger,

abounding in love and faithfulness, maintaining love to thousands,

and forgiving wickedness, rebellion and sin" (Exodus 34:6–7).

I praise you that you "hear when I call" on you

for my prodigal child (Psalm 4:3).

You are "my hope" and "my confidence" (Psalm 71:5).

I praise you that my prayers can change history,

because "all things are possible" with you (Mark 10:27).

So here she is, Father, the child you blessed me with,

a gift from your hand and your heart.

I pray that you will save her in absolutely every way imaginable!

And I praise you that you are "able to do immeasurably more than all"

I "ask or imagine" (Ephesians 3:20), because you are "the great God,

mighty and awesome" (Nehemiah 9:32).

Praise God for wanting a relationship with you, one where your prayers can even touch His heart! Thank God for the help and blessings that await you as you pray for your prodigal.

If I Should Die before She Wakes (I Pray the Lord Her Soul to Take)

All these people were still living by faith when they died.
They did not receive the things promised; they only
saw them and welcomed them from a distance.

HEBREWS 11:13

Father, I want so much to see my daughter come to you.

But what if it takes longer than my lifetime?

I will still live by faith,

and I will welcome your answer to my prayers "from a distance."

I'm amazed by how you treasure prayer, Father.

You keep our prayers before you in "golden bowls" (Revelation 5:8),
rising like incense.

Because you hold our prayers in your heart, you can even add years to
them that exceed our lives on earth.

How amazing you are, Father!

I come to you in faith again for my precious daughter.

Even if she doesn't come to you during my time on this earth,

I praise you that you will still be at work to answer my prayers
for her salvation.

How I long to see her soul awaken to you, Lord! To life, abundant
(John 10:10), eternal (John 3:15), and free (Revelation 22:17).

I'm reminded of your Word: "Wake up, sleeper, rise from the dead, and Christ will shine on you" (Ephesians 5:14).

Shine on her, Lord! Make your light shine in her heart to give her "the light of the knowledge of the glory of God in the face of Jesus Christ" (2 Corinthians 4:6 ESV).

Speak life to her, Lord, just like you did to Jairus' daughter (Luke 8:54).

Not a life that will end in death someday, but one that will "never die" (John 11:26).

Call her out of sin's deadly payback (Romans 6:23), into the kindness you have "prepared for those who love" you (1 Corinthians 2:9).

If I should die before she wakes, let me be standing near when you say to her in heaven, "Well done, good and faithful servant! . . . Come and share your master's happiness!" (Matthew 25:23).

Oh, that her life may be lived for the praise of your glory, Lord Jesus (Ephesians 1:12).

This is my prayer, and I offer it with faith and hope and love, because "I know that my redeemer lives" (Job 19:25).

I pray that she will know this too, Father.

And I praise you that *this* prayer lives on, because you do!

———

Praise God that because of His mercy and kindness, your prayers can outlive you. Then ask for faith to continue praying for your prodigal as long as it takes—even a lifetime!

Wanting What God Wants

Then the mother of Zebedee's sons came to Jesus
with her sons and, kneeling down, asked a favor of him.

MATTHEW 20:20

Ask most parents what they want for their child and you'll find they want good things: a successful career, a happy home, good health, a life with fewer challenges than they've had . . .

But what does God want?

Sometimes we don't give that question as much thought as we should. We naturally assume that God wants the "good things" we envision for our children and that our dreams for them are the same as His.

That's how the mother of James and John (the sons of Zebedee) saw it. Matthew writes that "the mother of Zebedee's sons came to Jesus with her sons and, kneeling down, asked a favor of him." When Jesus asked what she wanted, she answered, "Grant that one of these two sons of mine may sit at your right and the other at your left in your kingdom" (Matthew 20:20–21).

Why shouldn't she ask that? After all, Jesus had called her sons the "Sons of Thunder" (Mark 3:17 csb). They were ambitious and had great plans for the future and for the kingdom of God. And if anyone got in their way, like the time a Samaritan village didn't welcome Jesus, James and John wanted "to call fire down from heaven to destroy them" (Luke 9:54).

If anyone "had Jesus's back," it was the Sons of Thunder. But when Mom went to talk this over with Jesus, he responded, "You don't know what you are asking" (Matthew 20:22).

I don't want to be too hard on James and John's mother. I have a sneaking suspicion that they put Mom up to it. After all, certainly the strapping "Sons of Thunder" could have made Mom stand down. But they didn't. And when Jesus responded, he answered *them* directly, not her. Notice too that Matthew tells us that "when the ten heard about this, they were indignant *with the two brothers*" (Matthew 20:24). Mom doesn't get mentioned.

Still, she *did* ask. Maybe she got pulled into her sons' scheme. Any parent of a prodigal knows how easily *that* can happen. Her actions show that she loved her kids, like any good parent, and believed in them. Still, her encounter with Jesus raises a vital question: Do I want the same things for my child that God wants?

I find that if I'm not careful, I get caught up in the world's way of thinking: a successful future means the "right" schools, major, career path, and spouse. That's good as far as it goes, but it's too shortsighted when eternity comes into view. "What good is it for someone to gain the whole world, yet forfeit their soul?" (Mark 8:36). If my kids are successful heathens who look good from the world's point of view but will be separated from God for eternity, what kind of a future is *that*?

Nothing matters more than getting right with God. If I'm trying to shape their future with anything less in mind, I'm missing the mark by a mile and then some. But if I aim for what God wants, then there's always reason for hope.

When you're the parent of a prodigal child, you may feel like you have to settle for second best when it comes to the future. Maybe you've been "keeping score" with other kids his or her age, and it seems like your child is behind. Maybe your plans haven't worked out, and you're scrambling to come up with new ones. God once promised His people, "I know the plans I have for you . . . plans to prosper you and not to harm you, plans to give you hope and a future" (Jeremiah 29:11), and His heart hasn't changed.

The future He promises isn't limited to a lifespan. Not only can God open doors for our children on this earth, he can also open heaven.

Our prayer needs to be, "Father, help me to want what *you want* for my child. Help him to love you most of all!"

When that prayer is answered, then your son or daughter will be truly happy and have all that he or she needs. Not just for a few years on this earth but for every day to come, stretching on beyond forever, because "no eye has seen, . . . no ear has heard, . . . no human mind has conceived the things God has prepared for those who love him" (1 Corinthians 2:9).

Your possessions are never so safe as when you are willing to resign them, and you are never so rich as when you put all you have into the hand of God.

—CHARLES HADDON SPURGEON

Open Doors

Now God had caused the official to show favor and compassion to Daniel.

DANIEL 1:9

Some of my son's choices have affected his future, Father.

The missed opportunities, denied admissions, and closed doors would not have been so if he had applied the gifts that you've given him.

But that doesn't mean that he's missed the greatest opportunity of his life.

You are that opportunity, Lord! And you can make new opportunities for him.

More than wanting him to seek your hand and what you can do for him, I want him to seek your heart.

I pray that he will not miss all that you are.

Everything this earth has to offer pales in comparison with you and the beauty of a loving relationship with you.

"The heavens, even the highest heaven, cannot contain you" (1 Kings 8:27).

I ask that you would give him grace to comprehend deeply in his soul that "everyone is but a breath" (Psalm 39:5).

You promise, "I am with you to rescue and save you" (Jeremiah 15:20), and I pray that he will take that promise to heart.

But I also ask your help for his earthly future, Lord.

I pray you will help him to "give careful thought to the paths" for his feet and "be steadfast in all" his ways (Proverbs 4:26).

Just as you gave Daniel favor when his people were strangers in a country not their own, I ask that you will give my son wisdom to follow you and find your favor.

Just as you were "with Joseph so that he prospered" (Genesis 39:2) against all odds, I pray that he will be blessed in his work.

Only you can do this, Father. And I praise you that you can!

Please give him favor with employers and gatekeepers in a way that he will see your hand at work, and thank you for it.

Let doors open as he turns to you, so that he sees that "blessed is the one who trusts in the LORD, whose confidence is in him" (Jeremiah 17:7).

Please bless my son, Father!

Bless him with "a future hope" (Proverbs 23:18).

Bless him with "longing for your salvation" (Psalm 119:81).

Bless him with yourself!

———

Thank God that He can do more for your child's future in a single moment than you could do in a lifetime, through His favor and His love.

The Way Out

No temptation has overtaken you except what is common to
mankind. And God is faithful; he will not let you be tempted
beyond what you can bear. But when you are tempted,
he will also provide a way out so that you can endure it.

1 CORINTHIANS 10:13

She's had too many close calls lately, Lord.
The hot breath of temptation has been closing in and breathing down
    her neck.
She has walked into the situations willingly,
    knowing you'd have her take another path,
    and her feet "almost slipped" (Psalm 73:2).
I ask that your "power may rest on" her (2 Corinthians 12:9),
    so that she may "choose what pleases" you (Isaiah 56:4).
I pray you will give her *your* strength, Lord Jesus, so that she may
    have all she needs to stand strong in this challenging time
    (2 Corinthians 9:8).
I thank you that she faces no temptation that you do not understand,
    because you were "tempted in every way, just as we are,"
    yet you were "without sin" (Hebrews 4:15 csb).
I praise you that you are able "to sympathize with our weaknesses"
    in every way (Hebrews 4:15 csb).
Father, I cannot praise you enough for your promise that you will
    never let her "be tempted beyond what" she "can bear."
Each time, you will provide "a way out" (1 Corinthians 10:13).

Show her the way out, Lord! Mark it with a sign so big that she can't
   miss it! Better yet, stand right beside it and call her name.
"Who will rescue" her "from this body that is subject to death?"
   (Romans 7:24).
You will, Lord Jesus! And I love you for it.
You are the way out, Lord!
You are "the way and the truth and the life" (John 14:6).
You are the "living hope" that she needs (1 Peter 1:3).
Help her to "resist the devil" so that "he will flee from" her (James 4:7).
Restore her faith, Father, and make her
   "strong, firm and steadfast" (1 Peter 5:10).
I praise you that you are continually faithful!
I praise you that your love will never fail her or me!
Your "salvation will last forever"
   and your "righteousness will never fail" (Isaiah 51:6).
I place my trust in you today for both myself and my daughter,
   and I ask that your grace will set her free from temptation and sin.

———

**Talk with the Lord about an area of your life where He has helped you with
temptation, and thank Him for it. Then praise Him that He is able to do the
same for your prodigal, regardless of where he or she may struggle.**

DAY 17

For Open Eyes

I pray that the eyes of your heart may be enlightened in order
that you may know the hope to which he has called you,
the riches of his glorious inheritance in his holy people,
and his incomparably great power for us who believe.

EPHESIANS 1:18–19

He needs to see things in a new way, Father.

He needs a new and lasting vision for his life, and only you can give him that.

Father, I pray that "the eyes" of his "heart may be enlightened in order that" he "may know the hope" that comes from you alone.

May he know hope, and know you!

I pray that you, "the God of hope," will fill him "with all joy and peace" as he trusts in you, so that he may "overflow with hope by the power of the Holy Spirit" (Romans 15:13).

Bring him to a new place in his life, Lord! A place where he is "joyful in hope, patient in affliction, faithful in prayer" (Romans 12:12–13).

What a future awaits him when he turns to you!

Lord Jesus, you said, "The eye is the lamp of the body. If your eyes are healthy, your whole body will be full of light" (Matthew 6:22).

I long to see you shining through his eyes!

I long to hear your Word come from his mouth,

and to see you moving through his heart and hands.

That is the reason he was born, to know you and love you.

You "fashioned us for this very purpose" (2 Corinthians 5:5).

I pray he will "be made new in the attitude" of his mind,
and that he will "put on the new self, created to be like" you
"in true righteousness and holiness" (Ephesians 4:23–24).
Help him to understand that we are your "workmanship,
created in Christ Jesus for good works,"
which you "prepared ahead of time for us to do" (Ephesians 2:10).
His future is wide open with you, Lord!
You hold the future in your hands—and every blessing along with it.
Help him to understand that if he is on your side, he will have all he needs,
because "there is no wisdom, no insight, no plan that can
succeed against" you (Proverbs 21:30).
Everything that the devil has used to harm him will come to nothing,
because "the reason the Son of God appeared was to
destroy the devil's work" (1 John 3:8).
"Open his eyes, LORD, so that he may see" (2 Kings 6:17)
and choose to follow you today!

———

Think of a time that God has helped you see things in a way you never have before, and ask Him to give your prodigal a fresh, new comprehension of the need for a future with Him.

Father, Forgive

When they came to the place called the Skull, they crucified him there,
along with the criminals—one on his right, the other on his left.
Jesus said, "Father, forgive them, for they do not know what they
are doing." And they divided up his clothes by casting lots.

LUKE 23:33–34

No one is more forgiving than you, Lord. You are absolutely amazing!
After all you had suffered from our cruel hands,
    you even forgave us for torturing you.
Nothing can compare with your love. Nothing comes close.
What's more amazing is that *you* have *come close* to us!
You came near to show us how much you love us.
You died to set us free "from the law of sin and death" (Romans 8:2)
    and rose to give us life.
And while you were dying, you interceded with the Father for
    your murderers.
They really *didn't know* what they were doing, did they?
If they had understood, "they would not have crucified the
    Lord of glory" (1 Corinthians 2:8).
Thank you for your mercy, Lord Jesus. "I do not deserve" it (Luke 7:6),
    and I praise you for it.
There is such comfort in your love,
    such "tenderness and compassion" (Philippians 2:1).
You long for us with affection (Philippians 1:8),
    and my daughter really needs your compassion and affection now.

She's young and doesn't understand the consequences of her actions.

If only she would catch a glimpse of how wonderful you are,

then she couldn't help but love you!

Forgive her, Father. She does not know what she is doing (Luke 23:34).

I know that she must ask forgiveness for herself, and I pray that
she will!

I understand that "no one can say, 'Jesus is Lord,'
except by the Holy Spirit" (1 Corinthians 12:3).

So I ask that your Spirit will make your "light shine" in her heart
(2 Corinthians 4:6) and give her a fresh understanding of all
that you are.

Open her eyes, Lord Jesus, and show her "the way of peace" (Isaiah 59:8).

One day "we must all appear before" your "judgment seat"
(2 Corinthians 5:10), and I pray she will be ready!

Help me to help her in any way that I can.

Just as I was "at one time disobedient" to you and "have now received
mercy" (Romans 11:30), "may your mercy come quickly to meet"
her as well (Psalm 79:8).

Then, together we will tell how much you have done for us (Mark 5:19),
so others may know your mercy too!

————

**Have you ever said anything to your prodigal that you regret?
Thank God for His mercy that meets us in the most difficult places and
loves us despite our failings.**

God of the Second Chance

When they had finished eating, Jesus said to Simon Peter,
"Simon son of John, do you love me more than these?"
"Yes, Lord," he said, "you know that I love you."
Jesus said, "Feed my lambs."

JOHN 21:15

I love what you did for Peter, Lord.
After he had denied you three times (Matthew 26:34),
    you still forgave him and gave him another chance.
Thank you for your mercy, Lord!
Not only did you give Peter another chance but you also gave one to me.
And you continue to give me chances. You forgive me again and again.
My son needs your forgiveness too, Lord.
He needs the second chance that only you can give him.
You said, "You must be born again" (John 3:7),
    and I pray that he would be!
Make his "calling and election" sure (2 Peter 1:10).
Let there be no doubt in his mind that you have saved him and called
    him "to a holy life—not because of anything we have done,"
    but because of your "purpose and grace" (2 Timothy 1:9).
Father, I praise you that you want "*all people* to be saved
    and to come to a knowledge of the truth" (1 Timothy 2:4).
That includes my son!
I thank you that you want him to be saved and have placed the desire in
    my heart to pray for him.

I pray for a second chance for my son, just like you gave Peter.

I ask you, "Lord of the harvest," to "send out workers" into the "harvest field" (Matthew 9:38) that is my son's life.

Let him encounter your people wherever he goes,
and let them share your love with him in ways he cannot miss.

Let his heart be "burning within" (Luke 24:32)
when he encounters you speaking to him through your people.

Then open his eyes so that he may recognize you and turn his heart to you again.

Lord Jesus, you promised that "whoever comes to me I will never drive away" (John 6:37).

I pray he will come to you today!

Take some moments to praise God for the second (or third, or fourth . . .) chances He has given you, and thank Him for His mercy to you and your prodigal.

New Mercy!

Because of the Lord's great love we are not consumed, for his compassions
never fail. They are new every morning; great is your faithfulness.

LAMENTATIONS 3:22–23

Something good is coming, and I thank you for it,
      even though I don't know what it is yet!
But I know *you*, and your kindness is "new every morning."
Thank you, Lord, for your kindness to me and my daughter.
Thank you that when I am tired and come to the end of my strength,
      your strength keeps me going.
"My flesh and my heart may fail,"
      but you are "the strength of my heart" forever (Psalm 73:26).
"It is good to be near" you (Psalm 73:28).
It is good to know that I can come to you with every need
      and find you ready and waiting, tirelessly able to answer prayer.
Thank you for the incredible hope that you give.
"Whom have I in heaven but you?" (Psalm 73:25).
I will not give in to fear and doubt and worry, because you are with me.
You are "my helper" (Psalm 118:7),
      "my fortress and my deliverer" (2 Samuel 22:2).
I praise you that because of your "great love we are not consumed"
      (Lamentations 3:22).
You gave yourself "for us to redeem us from all wickedness"
      and to make us your "very own" (Titus 2:14).
I pray that new mercy will flow into my daughter's life with purpose and

power so that she may find the "better hope" that will enable her to "draw near" to you (Hebrews 7:19).

Then together we "will exalt you and praise your name, for in perfect faithfulness you have done wonderful things" (Isaiah 25:1).

We will find new things to praise you for that we haven't discovered yet, mercies still on the way from your loving hand.

Because of your kindness, I will renew my hope in you today.

You are "good to those whose hope is in" you (Lamentations 3:25).

I plead your mercy for my daughter, Lord, that she may soon find her heart's desire in you.

And I praise you that that day is coming, because your "compassions never fail." "Great is your faithfulness" (Lamentations 3:22–23).

———

Praise God that He knew exactly how we would sin before and even after we came to Him, and He chose to call us to himself anyway. Thank Him that His mercy is new each day.

Take Heart!

I have told you these things, so that in me you may have peace. In this world you will have trouble. But take heart! I have overcome the world.

JOHN 16:33

How good it is to hear you say, "take heart," Lord!

I praise you that I can "take heart" because you "have overcome the world"

and have overcome every obstacle my child and I will face.

We encounter nothing that you cannot handle!

No wonder your Word says, "Be strong and take heart,

all you who hope in the Lord" (Psalm 31:24).

My hope is in you, Lord!

I can be "greatly encouraged" because I "have this hope as an anchor for

the soul, firm and secure" (Hebrews 6:18–19).

You always live "to intercede" for us (Hebrews 7:25).

Even now while I am praying, you are bringing my needs before the Father.

He raised you "from the dead and [seated]" you "at his right hand . . .

far above every ruler and authority, power and dominion, and every

title given, not only in this age but also in the one to come"

(Ephesians 1:20–21 csb).

He "placed all things" under your feet (Ephesians 1:22),

even the troubles we face!

I praise you, Lord Jesus, because you meet our need and "save completely

those who come to God through" you (Hebrews 7:25–26).

I praise you for the promise that the Father will meet all our needs

"according to the riches of his glory in" you, Jesus (Philippians 4:19).

As I bring my son to you today, I think of what you told another young
   man: "Take heart, son; your sins are forgiven" (Matthew 9:2).
I long for him to hear you say that!
I long for him to ask for the forgiveness only you can give!
Lord Jesus, I pray that you will remove anything from his path
   that keeps him from coming to you.
Give him insight that "friendship with the world" will not get him
   anywhere but further away from you (James 4:4).
Help him understand that "the world and its desires pass away,
   but whoever does the will of God lives forever" (1 John 2:17).
I want him to live forever with you, Lord,
   and I take heart today because you want him to as well!
I take heart that he may one day have peace in you as I do
   because you answer prayer.
I pray he will receive your peace today, Lord.

————

Imagine Jesus sitting in front of you right now, telling you to "take heart."
Kneel in His presence, and worship Him for His perfect love.

The Running Father

*While he was still a long way off, his father saw him
and was filled with compassion for him; he ran to his son,
threw his arms around him and kissed him.*

LUKE 15:20

Dancing eyes, a cherub's face, and a shock of dark brown hair. I remember the first time I held my son in my arms. He was born quickly, twelve minutes after we arrived at the emergency room. There wasn't even time to hook up his mom's IV.

But all was well. Our baby boy was healthy and strong and mom was doing great. Just as we had done with his sister, before we left the hospital Cari and I enjoyed a quiet moment with our best friend, John. We took our son in our arms, bowed our heads, and gave him to God.

It would be the first of many prayers on his behalf.

All children need our prayers, especially those who pass through prodigal years. Geoffrey's childhood was idyllic. He was affectionate and loved to spend time with his family. We took trips, played games, and read good books and God's Word together. He was in Sunday school every Sunday of his life and received Jesus as his Savior at age seven. The years were full, and his childlike faith was sincere.

Little did we know that the sunshine of that season would give way to the clouds of another.

It was after midnight when the phone rang.

"Dad, it's me."

"Are you okay, Geoff?"

"I'm fine, but I'm spending the night at Andy's."

"That's not what we agreed to. You said you'd be home by midnight."

"I know, Dad. But . . . I really shouldn't drive, and Andy can't drive me home either."

I could tell by the sound of his voice that Geoffrey had been drinking. While he was making the right decision by staying off the roads, he knew better than to put himself in that situation to begin with.

When your child goes through prodigal years, you wonder where you went wrong as a parent. Not only do your children question you, *you* question *yourself*. You sometimes feel as if the whole world is watching, and you wonder if anyone truly understands.

Someone does.

When we were going through a particularly challenging time with Geoff, a friend pulled me aside after a meeting at our church. "I want you to know that I pray for you and your son every day," he said. Then he added: "I feel so guilty."

"Why do you feel guilty?" I asked, puzzled.

"Because I've never had to deal with prodigal children," he confided. "My daughters pretty much played by the rules. It's only now beginning to dawn on me how fortunate I was, and it wasn't because of anything I did or didn't do. I feel as if I've been spared, somehow. Kids," he shrugged, "make their own choices."

I wanted to hug him. I distinctly felt that God sent him at that moment with an insight I deeply needed to hear. His compassion was a gift from God, communicating to me the Father's understanding for my struggle with my son.

No one understands the struggle with prodigals better than our heavenly Father. The story of the prodigal son is our story and God's. Jesus told it on behalf of all sinners who need so desperately to come home to their Creator and discover the warmth of a loving relationship with Him.

The story of the prodigal son is the ultimate search and rescue. Jesus's mission was to "seek and to save the lost" (Luke 19:10). In the story, He paints a poignant picture of a father who does what was unthinkable for a parent in that culture at that time. Instead of standing at a distance while his son limped home, he looked for him and *ran* to him. Luke records Jesus's words: "While he was still a long way off, his father saw him and was filled with compassion for him; he ran to his son, threw his arms around him and kissed him" (Luke 15:20).

Jesus is God seeing us in the distance and looking on us with compassion. He is God running to us and throwing His arms around us. He is heaven's kiss welcoming the repenting sinner home.

No one cares more about prodigals than Jesus does. Jesus *loves* my prodigal son and welcomes my prayers for him. Jesus wants to restore him to the Father and welcome him home. He has called me to join in *His* search and rescue mission. Together, we're going after my son.

Jesus loves Geoff even more than I do. He loves him so much that He died to save him. And He longs for my prayers on Geoffrey's behalf.

After all, we gave Geoffrey to Jesus on the day he was born. And Jesus said, "Let the little children come to me, and do not hinder them, for the kingdom of heaven belongs to such as these" (Matthew 19:14). How could I do anything less than pray for my son?

Even though his way is dark and Geoffrey is far from home, God hasn't just left the light on for him. He's out on the front porch, watching, waiting, calling. And He's asked me to join Him.[4]

Our loved ones may spurn our appeals, reject our message, oppose our arguments, despise our persons—but they are helpless against our prayers.

—J. SIDLOW BAXTER

---

4. A few years after these words were written, Geoffrey would "come home" to faith in Jesus. We share his journey out of the "far country" in the book *Hope Lies Ahead,* which Geoff and I wrote together.

DAY 22

No Record of Wrongs

*Love is patient, love is kind. It does not envy, it does not boast,
it is not proud. It does not dishonor others, it is not self-seeking,
it is not easily angered, it keeps no record of wrongs.*

1 CORINTHIANS 13:4–5

I need the reminder, Lord, that love "keeps no record of wrongs."
I don't want to be the kind of parent who holds things against his child.
  Not anything. Not ever.
I know that you told me, "if you do not forgive others their sins,
  your Father will not forgive your sins" (Matthew 6:15).
How could I not forgive? You've forgiven me everything!
"You have put all my sins behind your back" (Isaiah 38:17).
Every sin I have ever committed has been taken away
  "as far as the east is from the west" (Psalm 103:12).
Thank you, Father, for loving me with such amazing love!
The more I live, the more I understand how much I need forgiveness
  and what a precious gift it is.
My daughter needs forgiveness too.
Someday she will need to know that I've forgiven her for any wrong
  she's done, even if she doesn't understand that yet. Please help me
  to do this, Lord.
In this moment, I pray for a heart that is willing to forgive. I want her to
  experience real forgiveness, from you and from me.
I want to leave anything she's done to me at the foot of the cross.

I want to put it behind us forever, and I ask your help to never bring it
up again.
I also ask your forgiveness, Father, for all of the times I've angrily reminded
her of her sins and mistakes, and recounted to her
my own personal "record of wrongs" (1 Corinthians 13:5).
Help me to have a heart like your own, Lord, "merciful and forgiving,
even though we have rebelled" (Daniel 9:9).
I know that claiming to forgive and forget is easier said than done,
because my tendency is to hold on to wrongs done against me.
Help me, Father, to let go of those hurts.
Please give me a heart that delights in grace and mercy.
I ask for grace to stand strong when I need to correct or discipline her,
because "better is open rebuke than hidden love" (Proverbs 27:5).
I also ask for grace to "gently [instruct], in the hope that" you will grant her
"repentance leading . . . to a knowledge of the truth" (2 Timothy 2:25).
When she comes to you and repents, what a beautiful moment that will be!
She will be like the woman who "loved much" (Luke 7:47 ESV) because
"her many sins have been forgiven" (Luke 7:47).
Just like mine.
And together, we will praise you for your mercy forever!

————

**Look up Psalm 139:23–24. Ask for God's help to examine your heart for
any areas where you find it difficult to forgive your prodigal, and ask for
grace to let go of any hard feelings from the past.**

For Perfect Love to Drive Out Fear

There is no fear in love. But perfect love drives out fear, because fear has to do with punishment. The one who fears is not made perfect in love.

1 JOHN 4:18

I want to be done with fear, Father.
I worry about my daughter because I love her,
    and it's hard for me not to worry.
But I know that I worry too much.
You told me not to "worry about tomorrow,
    for tomorrow will worry about itself."
You told me that "each day has enough trouble of its own" (Matthew 6:34).
I ask your forgiveness for borrowing trouble from tomorrow, Lord.
I know you have something far better in mind.
Help me draw near to you
    "with a sincere heart and with the full assurance that faith brings"
    (Hebrews 10:22).
I pray for grace to look forward to each new day, and ask that you fill me
    with "the faith and love that spring from the hope stored up for" me
    "in heaven" (Colossians 1:5).
I also ask that your perfect love will drive out fear from my life
    as I seek to lead my child to you.
Fill me with your love, Lord, in such a way that she sees you in me.
You are perfect love, Lord!

Help me to love her boldly and unselfishly, because "the Spirit" you
"gave us does not make us timid, but gives us power, love and
self-discipline" (2 Timothy 1:7).

Father, I praise you that "the Spirit" I "received does not make me"
a "[slave], so that" I "live in fear again;" but "the Spirit" I "received
brought about" my "adoption" to be your very own,
"And by him we cry 'Abba, Father'" (Romans 8:15).

Abba, Father, please bless my child!

I want to say, "I sought the LORD and he answered me;
he delivered me from all my fears" (Psalm 34:4).

Lord Jesus, I ask that your perfect love will drive out any fear
in my daughter's heart about coming to you.

Help her understand that knowing you is all about love,
which is so very different from any less-than-loving examples of
legalism or judgmentalism she may have seen along the way.

I pray that your love may be "made complete" in her so she
"will have confidence on the day of judgment" (1 John 4:17).

Let her live in love, because "whoever lives in love lives in" you
(1 John 4:16) and you in them.

May the wonder of all that you are bless my child
and draw her heart to you today!

What is your greatest worry for your prodigal? Talk with the Lord about it, and ask for His wisdom and peace.

Extra Miles

If anyone forces you to go one mile, go with them two miles.

MATTHEW 5:41

Sometimes I feel like I have some extra miles on me, Father.

There are days it seems like my child needs me to go the extra mile
more than once.

Thank you, Lord Jesus, that my child's needs are teaching me to serve him
in ways that you have served me.

You "did not come to be served, but to serve,
and to give" your life (Matthew 20:28).

I pray you will help me to serve my son in a way that will point him
to you.

Help me to have your attitude, Lord.
You took on "the very nature of a servant" (Philippians 2:7).

This isn't an easy road, but I accept it gratefully—
knowing that I'm following you.

I know by faith that this road comes out in a better place for him and for
me if I keep my eyes on you.

I pray that I will continue in "faith, established and firm," not moved
"from the hope held out in the gospel" (Colossians 1:23).

Because love "always perseveres" (1 Corinthians 13:7),
help me to take the steps I need to take to help my son
"without grumbling or arguing" (Philippians 2:14).

Help me to understand that "the end of a matter is better than its
beginning, and patience is better than pride" (Ecclesiastes 7:8).

Your eyes "range throughout the earth to strengthen those whose hearts are
fully committed to" you (2 Chronicles 16:9).

You are not only watching but you are also *with me.*

When I "pass through the waters" of difficult days, you have promised,
"I will be with you."

When I "pass through the rivers"—those days when we're in over our
heads—you have said, "they will not sweep over" us.

Even when I "walk through the fire" of trial or temptation or anger,
I "will not be burned" if I stay close to you (Isaiah 43:2).

You have promised to be with us always (Matthew 28:20).

Help me stay close to you in such a way that my son will learn to follow.

Let me walk humbly with you, knowing that I am an "unworthy" servant,
and I "have only done" my "duty" (Luke 17:10).

I ask for your unconditional love so I can love my son like you do, Father.

May he see your love in me and love you for it, forever and ever.

Thank the Lord that He "did not come to be served, but to serve" (Matthew
20:28). Ask for His love and strength to fill you as you attend to needs in
your prodigal's life.

For Grace to Abound at Home

And God is able to bless you abundantly,
so that in all things at all times, having all that you need,
you will abound in every good work.

2 CORINTHIANS 9:8

Sometimes I don't feel like I have much grace, Father.
My child knows just the right buttons to push
    and sometimes even seems to enjoy pushing them.
We need more grace at home, Lord!
There's been too much tension lately. Sometimes we are so focused on
    dealing with the negative that we lose sight of positive things.
Help me to "give thanks in all circumstances,"
    because that is exactly what you want me to do (1 Thessalonians 5:18).
Help me to never lose sight of the truth that "the joy of the LORD" is my
    strength (Nehemiah 8:10).
I need to be filled with your joy, Father!
I don't want my son to see my faith as simply a set of dos and don'ts.
I want him to see you in me!
Give me grace to grow all of the fruit of your Spirit:
    "love, joy, peace, forbearance, kindness, goodness,
    faithfulness, gentleness and self-control" (Galatians 5:22–23).
I pray you will also give him grace, Lord.
I trust your promise that you are "able to make all grace abound"
    (2 Corinthians 9:8 KJV), "in all things at all times."

Help me to "abound in every good work" (2 Corinthians 9:8 ESV),
so that he may see my "good deeds and glorify" you, Father
(Matthew 5:16).

I ask for grace to discipline him with the love and wisdom you alone can
give so that I may show him "the way to life" (Proverbs 6:23)
because your Word says "the one who loves" is "careful to discipline"
(Proverbs 13:24).

Help me to be careful "not to put any stumbling block or obstacle"
in his way (Romans 14:13).

I praise you that from your "abundance we have all
received one gracious blessing after another" (John 1:16 NLT).

I praise you that I have all that I need (2 Corinthians 9:8).

Help me to share those blessings with my son in every way,
so that your grace may be "poured out" on him "abundantly, along
with the faith and love" (1 Timothy 1:14) that you alone
can give!

———

"Where would I be without Jesus?" Reflect on that question before Him,
and thank Him for His grace for you. Ask Him to fill your heart afresh with
His Spirit (Ephesians 5:18).

You Promised!

But you have said, "I will surely make you prosper and will make your
descendants like the sand of the sea, which cannot be counted."

GENESIS 32:12

Thank you for Jacob, Lord. He reminded you of the promises you made
　　to him, and you blessed him because of it!

His boldness reminds me that you want me to pray your promises too.

Your promises build my faith and give me hope.

They help me remember your kindness and give me strength to go on.

Your Word makes it clear that your promises can be trusted:

　　"God is not a man, that he might lie, or a son of man,

　　that he might change his mind. Does he speak and not act,

　　or promise and not fulfill?" (Numbers 23:19 csb).

You keep your promises!

Because you are absolutely perfect, it is impossible for you to lie.

Your Word is filled with promises I want to pray again and again,
　　especially for my child.

Like Jacob, I want to pray what "you have said." After all, you
　　promised, Lord!

You said, "I will do whatever you ask in my name, so that the Father may
　　be glorified in the Son. You may ask me for anything in my name,
　　and I will do it" (John 14:13–14).

I know it would bring glory to the Father if my daughter gave her heart
　　to you, so I ask in your name, Lord Jesus, that she will!

You also tell me to have faith when I pray.

You said, "Whatever you ask for in prayer, believe that you have received it,
and it will be yours" (Mark 11:24).
I *do* believe that she will turn from the world and receive you,
because you promise to answer prayer!
I hold on to this promise from your Word: "Believe in the Lord Jesus,
and you will be saved—you and your household" (Acts 16:31).
I look forward to the day when everyone in my home will praise you
together, Lord.
I believe this is entirely possible for you to accomplish,
and I hang on to your promise that "everything is possible
for one who believes" (Mark 9:23).
Thank you that I can rely on your Word because you are reliable.
You said about your Word, "It will not return to me empty,
but will accomplish what I desire and achieve the purpose
for which I sent it" (Isaiah 55:11).
I know you've given me your Word so I can fill my heart and my life with it.
I will "trust in your word" (Psalm 119:42), and you with it!
Help me to "study the Scriptures diligently" (John 5:39)
in order to know you better and love you more.
Then I will keep finding promises to pray,
and praise you all the more when you keep them!

———

**What are some of your favorite promises from God's Word? Take a moment
to thank God for them, and then pray them for your prodigal.**

Thank You

Children are a gift from the LORD;
they are a reward from him.

PSALM 127:3 NLT

I don't think I've said "thank you" enough lately, Lord.
Your Word reminds me that children are a blessing from you,
  and I take that to heart.
I'd like to thank you again for the blessing of my son.
He is your own beautiful and unique creation.
There will never be anyone exactly like him.
I praise you because he is "fearfully and wonderfully made;
  your works are wonderful, I know that full well" (Psalm 139:14).
I thank you for my son's good characteristics.
I even thank you for the strength of his will and look forward to the day
  that it will be used to serve you with devotion and resolve.
I thank you for the things I sometimes take for granted:
  the blessings of health, and food, and a roof over our heads.
Even though times are challenging right now,
  I don't want to stop saying thank you.
Your Word tells me to "give thanks in all circumstances, for this is
  God's will for you in Christ Jesus" (1 Thessalonians 5:18).
I thank you especially for your patience with my son, and with me.
Help me to "bear in mind that our Lord's patience means salvation"
  (2 Peter 3:15).

Though my son hasn't turned his heart to you yet,
>I thank you that you are still waiting, still bearing with him,
>still holding out your hand.

O, Father, I pray that his salvation will come soon!

Thank you, Father, for the hope of your salvation.
>Thank you for the wonder and beauty of all that you are.

Your patience with me and my son gives me reason for hope.

Even though others may doubt you are near, I hang on to you and
>trust in you.

Thank you, Father, for the kindness you have shown us in so many ways!

Your goodness never ends: "Your plans for us are too numerous to list.
>You have no equal.

If I tried to recite all your wonderful deeds, I would never come to the
>end of them" (Psalm 40:5 NLT).

You are always faithful,
>"a faithful God who does no wrong" (Deuteronomy 32:4).

Thank you for your promise that "though the mountains be shaken and
>the hills be removed, yet my unfailing love for you will not be shaken"
>(Isaiah 54:10).

"How priceless is your unfailing love!" (Psalm 36:7).

I thank you for the blessing of a child I dearly love, Lord,
>and I praise you that you love him even more than I do.

"Show us your unfailing love, LORD,
>and grant us your salvation" (Psalm 85:7).

Take a moment to remember something you are genuinely grateful for about your prodigal, and thank God for him or her.

DAY 28

Blessed without Knowing It

When Jacob awoke from his sleep, he thought,
"Surely the LORD is in this place, and I was not aware of it."

GENESIS 28:16

You never cease to surprise me, Lord.
There have been many times when you were at work in my son's life,
    and I didn't know it.
I'd like to thank you for those times, Father, especially for the ones that are
    happening right now that I'm unaware of.
You told Nicodemus, "The wind blows wherever it pleases. You hear its
    sound, but you cannot tell where it comes from or where it is going. So
    it is with everyone born of the Spirit" (John 3:8).
You are at work in ways that I may not see for years.
Nothing escapes you; you have heard my prayers for my son and are
    lovingly responding.
Your faithfulness makes me want to pray all the more.
I praise you that you never stop working, Lord.
You "will not grow tired or weary,"
    and "no one can fathom" your understanding (Isaiah 40:28).
When I'm feeling worn out, it helps to remember that you never grow
    tired!
My son can run from you only so long, because "even youths grow tired
    and weary, and young men stumble and fall" (Isaiah 40:30).
Catch him, Lord! Be there when he falls to his knees and calls out
    to you.

I thank you that you will be there to lift him up and hold him close,
just like I used to do when he fell as a boy.

"Speak tenderly" to him that his sin "has been paid for" (Isaiah 40:2),
and lead him home to you.

You have ways to reach him that I have not thought of, Father.

You do "great things beyond our understanding" (Job 37:5).

How many blessings have I not thought of?

How wonderful you are, Lord! "How great is the goodness you have stored
up for those who fear you.

You lavish it on those who come to you for protection, blessing them before
the watching world" (Psalm 31:19 NLT).

Just like Jacob, who realized that your presence surrounded him,
I pray you will awaken my son to the beauty of your presence.

Let him hear you say, "I am with you and will watch over you wherever you
go" (Genesis 28:15).

As you did with me, bring him to the understanding that your blessing
reaches further than he could ever imagine, and let him praise you for
it forever.

———————

**Read Ephesians 1:18, then pray that your prodigal will see God in a way he
or she never has before.**

The Stretcher of Faith

*When Jesus saw their faith, he said to the
paralyzed man, "Son, your sins are forgiven."*

MARK 2:5

My mother had the spiritual gift of faith (1 Corinthians 12).

When I was a teenager, few things bothered me more.

"Just trust God," she'd tell me. "He will take care of you." Sometimes she'd smile and break into song, finishing her thoughts with a hymn.

It used to drive me up a wall. I can still hear my protests as I'd stomp off: "It isn't that simple, Mom!"

But to her it was. She knew God was faithful. He had always taken care of her. During the Great Depression when her father died young and through the Second World War and the Korean War when Dad was frequently in harm's way and even missing in action, Mom held on to faith, and God held on to her.

Mom suffered from Alzheimer's disease in her final years. Dad had cared for her until he died, and then she came to live with Cari and me until she needed additional care. There were blessings in those days we never saw coming. Though Mom had forgotten much, the hymns she so dearly loved remained. Sometimes I'd sing to her and she'd remember the words with surprising clarity and join in.

At the time of Dad's death, the family agreed to sell Dad and Mom's home to fund Mom's extended care needs. Dad had bought the house fully furnished as part of an estate sale when I was in seventh grade, and because Mom was facing an illness that would last for several years and money was limited, all of the contents of the house would be appraised and sold.

Once again, God came through for Mom. At the appraisal, two paintings were discovered. They were the work of Granville Redmond, a California Impressionist artist. Together they sold at auction for more than $400,000, funding Mom's care to the end of her days.

Even when Alzheimer's assaulted her mind and her memory, God showed His faithfulness to her through those paintings in a way that I would never forget. It *changed* me. Sometimes I can hear my mother's own words coming out of my mouth to my own children: "Just trust God. He will take care of you."

Faith must be caught as well as taught. Parents of prodigal kids need to pray that their faith will be evident to their children. Children need to catch their parents actively believing and see their parents' faith lived out.

Mark and Luke tell a striking story of Jesus "catching people in the act" of faith. Four men brought a friend who was paralyzed to Jesus for healing. When they couldn't find a way through the crowd, they climbed up on the roof of the home where Jesus was teaching, removed some tiles, and lowered the man "right in front of Jesus" (Luke 5:19). Mark and Luke both write that "when Jesus saw *their* faith," he healed their friend (Mark 2:5, Luke 5:20).

Notice that both Mark and Luke mention more than just the faith of the man who was healed. Jesus saw "*their* faith," indicating the faith of his friends. When the man was paralyzed and could do little for himself, the active faith of those around him made all the difference.

When we pray for our prodigal kids, we carry them on stretchers of faith to Jesus. We do the heavy lifting, but they receive the benefit. They may be entirely passive or even actively resisting us, but Jesus sees *our* faith as we bring them to Him.

Jim Cymbala writes of his daughter Chrissy's return after a long prodigal season.[5] One Tuesday evening, God impressed upon the people in the

---

5. Cymbala, *Fresh Wind, Fresh Fire*, 64–65.

church he serves (The Brooklyn Tabernacle) to intercede passionately for his daughter. He came home that evening and told his wife, "It's over with Chrissy. You would have had to be in the prayer meeting tonight. I tell you, if there's a God in heaven, this whole nightmare is finally over."

Two days later, his daughter came home to her family and back to God. She asked one question over and over: "Daddy . . . *who was praying for me? Who was praying for me?*"

That Tuesday night God moved in her soul and showed her she was headed toward destruction, all the while affirming His love for her. Somehow, she *knew* He had used the passionate prayers of His people to bring her back to Him.

Our prodigal kids desperately need us to lift them to Jesus on the stretcher of prayer. Even if they don't have faith, He will see ours. And *they* will be blessed because of it.

The great battle of our spiritual lives is "Will you believe?"
It is not, "Will you try harder?" or "Can you make yourself Worthy?"
It is squarely a matter of believing that God will do what only he can do.

—**JIM CYMBALA**

Snatched from the Fire

Be merciful to those who doubt;
save others by snatching them from the fire.

JUDE 22-23

He's been playing with fire, Lord, and he doesn't even know it.
He thinks he's having a good time doing whatever he wants to do.
He doesn't realize that "there is a way that appears to be right,
    but in the end it leads to death" (Proverbs 14:12).
Father, the thought of my son being anywhere near the vicinity of
    "the fire of hell" (Matthew 18:9) is almost too painful for me to bear.
But because I am shielded by your power (1 Peter 1:5),
    I will face that fear and go after him with this prayer.
I ask that you will use me in any way you want to save my son.
    Whatever it takes, Lord!
God, help me to snatch him "from the fire."
I can't do it on my own. But "I can do all things through him
    who strengthens me" (Philippians 4:13 ESV).
Thank you that I'm not alone in this, Lord. I am depending on your
    strength.
We're going after him together, because you are
    "with me like a mighty warrior" (Jeremiah 20:11).
The foes we face may be many.
But I remember what your people prayed in a past battle:
    "We do not know what to do, but our eyes are on you"
    (2 Chronicles 20:12).

I look to you for my son's salvation, and for you to overcome every foe.
Rebuke the adversary, Lord (Zechariah 3:2).
Your Word says that the children of believers "are holy" (1 Corinthians 7:14).
I know my son still must turn to you to be saved, but I also know that
    the adversary steps onto holy ground to pursue my son
    and takes aim at someone both of us love.
Lord Jesus, when Peter confessed, "You are the Messiah, the Son of the
    living God" (Matthew 16:16), you replied that "the gates of Hades
    will not overcome" that confession (Matthew 16:18).
I confess you as Lord as well!
Break down those gates, Lord! Pull my son from the fire while there is
    still time!
I pray that my son will repent of his sins
    and confess you as his Lord and Savior today.
May today be the time of your favor.
May today be "the day of salvation" (2 Corinthians 6:2).

———

Talk with God about skipping a meal so you can fast and pray for your prodigal's salvation. Consider also asking a spouse or friend to join you at the same time so you can support one another in prayer.

DAY 30

A Softer Heart

I will give you a new heart and put a new spirit in you;
I will remove from you your heart of stone and give you a
heart of flesh. And I will put my Spirit in you.

EZEKIEL 36:26–27

Lord, I've read how you "hardened the heart of Pharaoh" (Exodus 14:8)
    to set your people free.
Since you hardened his heart to bless your people,
    may I ask you to soften my son's?
You promise in your Word,
    "I will give you a new heart and put a new spirit in you."
What a blessing that would be for my son!
I pray you will move in his heart today in a fresh and powerful way.
His heart has been "hardened by sin's deceitfulness" (Hebrews 3:13),
    but it wasn't always that way.
There was a time when he was open to you. He received you,
    and your love was at work in him in a beautiful way.
But his faith has been "choked" by this world (Luke 8:7).
"Life's worries, riches and pleasures" have led him astray
    and held him back from growing strong in you (Luke 8:14).
"But with you there is forgiveness" (Psalm 130:4).
There is still hope for him, and I praise you for it!
Just as Solomon prayed that you would turn the Israelites' hearts to you
    (1 Kings 8:58), may you turn my son's heart to you as well!

I pray he will no longer "waver between two opinions" (1 Kings 18:21)
but love you wholeheartedly.

When he turns to you, I know you will welcome him, because that is
your heart!

Give him "an undivided heart and put a new spirit" in him (Ezekiel 11:19).

"Remove from" him his "heart of stone and give" him
"a heart of flesh" (Ezekiel 36:26).

Then let your grace be with his spirit, Lord Jesus (Philemon 25),
and may he know that "your Name is near" (Psalm 75:1).

May he trust that you will "never leave us nor forsake us" (1 Kings 8:57).

I pray that he will walk in all your ways, to love you and to serve you with
all his heart and with all his soul (Deuteronomy 10:12).

Let his heart be "steadfast," O God (Psalm 57:7).

Let each new day bring him hope of "your unfailing love" (Psalm 143:8).

His heart is in your hands, Father, and so is mine.

I long to see him filled with your love, Lord, and I know that you
do too.

I pray that he will give his heart to you today!

———

How has God changed your own heart with His love? Thank Him for this, and ask Him to do the same for your prodigal.

DAY 31

Whoever

For God so loved the world that he gave his one and only Son,
that whoever believes in him shall not perish but have eternal life.

JOHN 3:16

"Whoever."

Thank you for including that word in John 3:16, Lord. I love what
   it means.

It tells me that regardless of what we have done, if we come to you and
   "confess our sins," you are "faithful and just and will forgive us our sins
   and purify us from all unrighteousness" (1 John 1:9).

That means that my child can find forgiveness.

Even though others may write her off for the things she's done,
   if she turns to you, you will receive her. That is all that matters.

"Whoever"! That word gives me so much hope.

I praise you, Lord Jesus, for what you have done for us.
   Because of "the joy set before" you, you "endured the cross,
   scorning its shame, and sat down at the right hand of
   the throne of God" (Hebrews 12:2).

Does that mean *we* are part of that joy? It must!

You said that the reason you came was
   "to seek and to save the lost" (Luke 19:10).

You also said that if we obediently follow you,
   your "joy may be in" us, and our "joy may be complete" (John 15:11).

I want my daughter to know your joy so much, Lord!
   There's nothing like knowing you.

I pray she will come to understand that she has an emptiness within her
that only you can fill.
She tries to fill it with pleasures and distractions,
but they only leave her looking for more.
Father, I ask today that you will show her again how much you
love her.
You love her so much that you gave your "one and only Son"!
Break through her distractions and show her the pointlessness
of going her own way and living apart from you.
Remind her that whoever does that will "perish" because "the wages of
sin is death, but the gift of God is eternal life in Christ Jesus"
(Romans 6:23).
I pray for life for my daughter, Lord! The life you alone can give!
Use this prayer in your search-and-rescue mission to pull her up to the
safety of your love. And use *me*, Father, any way you desire.
I know that you've given my daughter to me for this reason—
not only for the personal, earthly blessing of being a parent,
but also because you want to use me for the salvation of her
eternal soul.
No matter what she's done, you still love her with an amazing love,
and I thank you that you will respond to every prayer for her
"out of the goodness of your love" (Psalm 69:16).

**Think about answers to prayer that you've seen in your life. Then praise
God for the privilege of prayer and the role your prayers can have in your
prodigal's salvation.**

A Better Attitude

*You were taught, with regard to your former way of life, to put off
your old self, which is being corrupted by its deceitful desires;
to be made new in the attitude of your minds; and to put on
the new self, created to be like God in true righteousness and holiness.*

EPHESIANS 4:22–24

When she looks in the mirror, Father, what does she see?

Does she see only what's on the outside? Help her to take a deeper
look, Lord.

Give her grace to look beyond her physical reflection and into
her heart.

She needs a new attitude, Lord. She needs the encouragement that can
come only from "faith and hope" in you (1 Peter 1:21).

I pray you will help her to "put off" her old self,
"which is being corrupted by its deceitful desires,"
and bloom into the person you long for her to be.

Give her a makeover on the inside, Lord!

Let her be "made new in the attitude" of her mind,
so that she looks forward to life in a way she never
has before.

Help her understand that with your power and love at work in her heart
and mind, her "new self" will be the person you intended her to
be all along—"created to be like" you.

I praise you, Father, that you love my daughter,
and that you love her too much to leave her just as she is.

You want her to be transformed into your likeness (2 Corinthians 3:18),
  a daughter of the "King of glory" (Psalm 24:10).
Let there be no doubt as to the family resemblance:
  may everything about her remind others of you!
Thank you, Jesus, that you were made like us "in every way" (Hebrews 2:17),
  so that we could be made like you.
Thank you, Lord Jesus, that you shared in our humanity
  so that by your death you would destroy "him who holds the power
  of death . . . and free those who all their lives were held in slavery"
  (Hebrews 2:14–15).
Set my daughter free, Lord!
Free to love you, and free to live!
Free to repent of her sins and make a brand-new beginning.
Free to reach her full potential and be a blessing to others.
Free to one day run barefoot in the New Jerusalem (Revelation 21:2),
  because she was "born again" in you (John 3:3).

————

Romans 12:2 reminds us to "be transformed by the renewing of [our] mind."
Ask God to help your prodigal deeply desire to make a new beginning with
Him, and ask Him to give you fresh ideas as you pray.

DAY 33

Friends, and a Friend

One who has unreliable friends soon comes to ruin,
but there is a friend who sticks closer than a brother.

PROVERBS 18:24

I pray for my son, Lord. He needs wisdom in choosing his friends.
He needs good friends, Father. Friends who know you and have a sincere
faith, who will be faithful to you and to him, and who
will "reject the wrong and choose the right" (Isaiah 7:15).
I pray you will protect him from friends who would lead him astray,
because "bad company corrupts good character" (1 Corinthians 15:33).
Give my son the strength to "not go along with them" (Proverbs 1:15).
I ask for friends who will be attracted to his good qualities,
and who will encourage him to develop them.
I ask for friends who will love "whatever is true, whatever is noble,
whatever is right, whatever is pure, whatever is lovely,
whatever is admirable" (Philippians 4:8).
You know he has friends I don't care for, Father. But I also know that you
love them, no matter how far from you they may be.
So I pray for my son's friends who need to know you.
Save them, Lord! And let the work of your Spirit in their lives
draw my son's heart to you as well.
You are the "friend who sticks closer than a brother."
You have promised "I will never leave you nor forsake you" (Joshua 1:5).
You have said, "I have made you and I will carry you;
I will sustain you and I will rescue you" (Isaiah 46:4).

He needs rescuing, Lord, and you alone can do that.
Help him understand that he needs a friend like you most of all,
    and to turn to you with all his heart.
Thank you for being my friend, Father.
    "Your love is better than life" (Psalm 63:3).
"Because you are my help, I sing in the shadow of your wings" (Psalm 63:7).
I look forward to what you will do in my son's life
    and in the lives of his friends.
"I will thank you forever, because you have done it" (Psalm 52:9 esv),
    because you "heard my cry for mercy when I called to you for help"
    (Psalm 31:22).
"Great is your faithfulness" (Lamentations 3:23).

———

Think of some of the people Jesus befriended whom others would not get close to, and thank Him that He desires to be your prodigal's friend.

Innocence Found

"Come now, let us settle the matter," says the LORD.
"Though your sins are like scarlet, they shall be as white as snow;
though they are red as crimson, they shall be like wool."

ISAIAH 1:18

I praise you, Lord, because you are innocence found.
You are "the Lamb of God, who takes away the sin of the world!" (John 1:29).
You are the "lamb without blemish" (1 Peter 1:19).
Your "works are perfect," and all your "ways are just."
  You are "a faithful God who does no wrong" (Deuteronomy 32:4).
You are sinlessness and wisdom together, absolute perfection!
Lord Jesus, how you could be "tempted in every way, just as we are,"
    yet "did not sin" (Hebrews 4:15) amazes me
    and makes me want to worship you all the more.
You are not only entirely sinless but you also restore innocence to us
    because you are "able to save completely those who come to God
    through" you (Hebrews 7:25).
My daughter needs to be saved completely, Lord.
She needs the gift of your forgiveness and the washing away of
    her guilt.
No one can remove sin's stain like you so we may be
    "set free from sin" (Romans 6:22) and "born again" (1 Peter 1:23)
    to a completely new life!
You promise, "Though your sins are like scarlet,
    they shall be as white as snow" (Isaiah 1:18).

Father, I pray that you and my daughter will "reason together" (Isaiah 1:18 RSV) and that she will long for the innocence you freely give.

May she ask and find your full forgiveness.

Deep in her spirit, let her hear you say, "I, even I, am he who blots out your transgressions, for my own sake, and remembers your sins no more" (Isaiah 43:25).

Let her "[escape] the corruption in the world caused by evil desires" (2 Peter 1:4), and be "washed," "sanctified," and "justified in the name of the Lord Jesus Christ and by the Spirit" (1 Corinthians 6:11).

Through your Spirit, let her hear in her heart the hope you have for her: "Forget the former things; do not dwell on the past. See, I am doing a new thing!" (Isaiah 43:18–19).

You are the God of new beginnings!

You can set her feet on a new path!

"The crooked roads shall become straight," and "the rough ways smooth" (Luke 3:5)! Make it so, Lord!

Let her be part of the bride of Christ, "without stain or wrinkle or any other blemish, but holy and blameless" in every way (Ephesians 5:27)!

Loving Father, may your gift of innocence be hers today!

———

Praise God that no matter what your prodigal has said or done, a new beginning is still possible with Him.

DAY 35

Praise Because You've Been There

As he approached Jerusalem and saw the city, he wept over it and said, "If you, even you, had only known on this day what would bring you peace—but now it is hidden from your eyes."

LUKE 19:41–42

You've been there, haven't you, Lord Jesus?
You know what it's like to look with longing on those you love,
  hoping and praying that they will turn their hearts to the Father.
You wept over Jerusalem more than once, didn't you?
On another day you looked over the city and said, "I have longed to gather
  your children together, as a hen gathers her chicks under her wings,
  and you were not willing" (Matthew 23:37).
You "reared children and brought them up,
  but they have rebelled against" you (Isaiah 1:2).
My heart goes out to you, Lord. You know exactly how I feel
  about my son.
"All my longings lie open before you, Lord;
  my sighing is not hidden from you" (Psalm 38:9).
  I want such good things for him!
I long for him to see you as you are,
  and to know your joy deep in his heart.
I long for him to find the peace that only you can give.
But just like Jerusalem, at the moment "it is hidden from" his eyes.

If I have such longing about one child,

    I can only begin to imagine how you feel about an entire city!

You understand completely what is like to have a prodigal child.

Some people cannot understand because they haven't had one,

and they have no idea of the heartbreak.

I've felt the condemnation of their glances

    and the weight of the words they do not say.

Thank you, Father, that you are not that way.

You know what it's like to have a world full of prodigal children,

    and only one child who did what was right—your Son, our Savior!

You love us so much that you "gave him up for us all" (Romans 8:32).

I praise you that you did not send your "Son into the world to condemn

    the world, but to save the world through him" (John 3:17).

Thank you for not looking on my son with condemnation but

    with love.

You long for him to come to you just as you longed for the people

    of Jerusalem.

You long for him to come to you with a depth I cannot begin

    to fathom.

I pray that he will, Lord, for your sake and for his.

I pray he will understand that "now is the time" of your favor,

    "now is the day of salvation" (2 Corinthians 6:2),

    and give his heart fully and freely to you!

———

Thank Jesus that He truly understands the pain you are going through with your prodigal, and simply rest for a moment in His perfect love.

Just Say the Word

When Jesus had entered Capernaum, a centurion came to him,
asking for help. "Lord," he said, "my servant lies at home paralyzed,
suffering terribly." Jesus said to him, "Shall I come and heal him?"
The centurion replied, "Lord, I do not deserve to have you come under
my roof. But just say the word, and my servant will be healed." . . .
When Jesus heard this, he was amazed and said to those following him,
"Truly I tell you, I have not found anyone in Israel with such great
faith." . . . Then Jesus said to the centurion, "Go! Let it be done just as
you believed it would." And his servant was healed at that moment.

MATTHEW 8:5–13

When we were in high school, one of my older brothers made a decision he would regret. He decided to try streaking.

One sunny Saturday afternoon when Mom was quietly reading, he summoned his twin and me to the front door. Wearing only a towel, he explained his plan carefully.

"I'm going to streak out to the curb, and you guys keep watch for Mom. After I count to three, you run to the other door and make sure I don't come in that way if she's close by. Got it?"

His twin and I nodded our heads in agreement: "Okay!"

"One . . . two . . . three . . . NOW!"

The towel dropped.

He bounded out the door.

And we *locked* it behind him.

We didn't only lock *that* door. While he was enjoying his "nature walk," we locked every door to the house. Within a minute, he was back and trying desperately to open a bolted door.

The pounding on the door that followed sounded like something out of a biblical parable. But all the noise just made matters worse. It made his brothers yell all the louder, "MOM, SOMEBODY'S AT THE DOOR!"

Mom *did* answer the door. But my brother was never grounded for his misadventure. After she stopped laughing, I think she felt that the punishment already given had met the crime.

Sometimes our kids trust the wrong people and it gets them in trouble. But we find a beautiful example of who *can* be trusted in the story of the centurion with the sick servant (Matthew 8:5–13).

Moments after Jesus entered Capernaum, "a centurion came to him, asking for help" (Matthew 8:5). His servant was deathly ill, paralyzed and suffering. Immediately Jesus promised, "I will come and heal him" (Matthew 8:7 ESV).

The centurion's response was amazing: "Lord, I do not deserve to have you come under my roof. But just say the word, and my servant will be healed" (Matthew 8:8).

The centurion, charged with the responsibility of at least a hundred soldiers under his command, was used to giving orders. He represented Caesar's authority over the province where he served, and disobedience to him was the same as defying the emperor.

He saw the same kind of authority in Jesus. Only Jesus's authority came from God, and the centurion knew it. That's why he said, "I do not deserve to have you come under my roof."

There are only two incidents in Scripture where Jesus is described as being "astonished" or "amazed" (the other is with the people in his hometown in Mark 6:6). Both instances had to do with faith. In his hometown, it was the *lack* of faith that amazed him and kept him from performing miracles.

Here was a Gentile, a man representing an occupying foreign army. But he believed that Jesus could do what he promised from a distance: "Just say the word, and my servant will be healed."

That kind of faith evoked an amazing response from Jesus: "Go! Let it be done just as you believed it would."

Something happened here that we must not miss. Instead of doing what He originally said He would do, Jesus did what the man *believed* He could do. And Matthew writes that "his servant was healed at that moment" (Matthew 8:13).

What do you believe that Jesus can do for your prodigal son or daughter? It's easy to become discouraged and allow our circumstances to shape our faith (or our lack of it). But what if we take the centurion's experience of Jesus to heart? What if we believe all the more in the greatness and power of our Savior? Just a word from Him can change our prodigal's life forever.

What if we trust Jesus *more*, and believe that He is "able to do immeasurably more than all we ask or imagine" (Ephesians 3:20)? What changes might occur in our child's life as a result?

One thing is certain: Jesus *loves* that kind of faith.

And wouldn't you love to amaze Jesus?

The prince of darkness grim,
we tremble not for him.
His rage we can endure,
for lo! his doom is sure.
One little word shall fell him.

—MARTIN LUTHER,
"A MIGHTY FORTRESS IS OUR GOD"

For Chains to Fall

He brought them out of darkness, the utter darkness,
and broke away their chains.

PSALM 107:14

You've broken so many chains, Lord!
You did it for Joseph in prison (Genesis 41:14).
You did when you set your people free from Pharaoh (Exodus 12:51).
You did if for Daniel (Daniel 6:23)
    and Shadrach and Meshach and Abednego (Daniel 3:26).
You brought your people out of Babylon (Ezra 2:1).
You even sent an angel to Peter in prison,
    "and the chains fell off Peter's wrists" (Acts 12:7).
My son has his chains too, Lord.
They're not made of iron. They're made from sins he forged of his own free
    will, thinking they would bring him more freedom.
They've done anything but that.
    They've only kept him from coming closer to you.
You promised that "if the Son sets you free,
    you will be free indeed" (John 8:36).
Your Word says, "The LORD sets prisoners free" (Psalm 146:7).
Set him free, Lord! He needs you to break his chains.
I ask to hear the sound of chains falling with a dull thud,
    never to be put on again.
I long to hear my son say, "The LORD has done great things" for me,
    and I am "filled with joy" (Psalm 126:3).

I long for him to say to you, "I run in the path of your commandments,
for you have broadened my understanding" (Psalm 119:32).

Please give him grace to understand that obedience to you is the best kind
of freedom, because it enables him to be the person you created him
to be.

Help him to see that when he is conformed "to the pattern of this world"
(Romans 12:2), it is the worst kind of slavery:
"bondage to decay" (Romans 8:21).

Father, I know only part of the challenges he's facing, but you know all
of them.

I ask that you will break his chains link by link, so that he will turn to you.

I pray that the things that once captivated him will lose their lure,
and he will understand they are "the devil's trap" (1 Timothy 3:7).

I pray he will come to his "senses and escape from the trap of the devil,
who has taken" him "captive to do his will" (2 Timothy 2:26).

You've set so many free, Father! I ask that you do the same for my son.

Let him say of you, "My heart trusts in him, and he helps me.
My heart leaps for joy" (Psalm 28:7).

Let him leap, Lord! A leap of faith out of his chains and straight
to you.

————

**What is the greatest "chain" in your prodigal's life right now? Praise God
that it is not too strong for Him!**

For an Honest Answer

An honest answer is like a kiss on the lips.

PROVERBS 24:26

I remember honest answers, Lord.

When my son was little, he'd say things so truthfully.

I loved those moments! The innocent questions an adult would never ask,
the just-the-facts statements that left no room for doubt.

I pray for honesty for my son, Father. He's been struggling with that recently.

Help him to work hard to keep his
"conscience clear before God and man" (Acts 24:16).

I ask that you will help him to understand the damage that dishonesty does
to his relationships with others.

Help him to grasp the fact that "whoever walks in integrity walks securely,
but whoever takes crooked paths will be found out" (Proverbs 10:9).

Father, please give him grace to *want* to be a man of integrity
who can look others in the eye and "speak the truth" (Zechariah 8:16).

Help me to be honest with him and to resist the temptation to
compromise the truth in any way, simply because he hasn't been
honest with me.

I ask that he will understand that in order to be trusted,
he has to be trustworthy.

He wants me to trust him. I pray that you will help him see the disconnect
between what he wants and his actions.

Help him to become "blameless and pure," a child of God "without fault in
a warped and crooked generation" (Philippians 2:15).

Touch his heart, Lord, so he can understand what you meant when you
said that "whoever can be trusted with very little can also be trusted
with much" (Luke 16:10).
Help him to be honest in the little things as well as the larger ones.
I know he lies to me sometimes because he knows
that I'll disapprove of something he's done.
Father, please help him understand that though he may hide from me,
he can never hide from you.
"You are the God who sees" (Genesis 16:13).
You "desire truth in the innermost being" (Psalm 51:6 NASB).
You told us that we must give an account
for every "careless word" we have spoken (Matthew 12:36).
"I know, my God, that you test the heart and are pleased with integrity"
(1 Chronicles 29:17).
I pray that he will walk in the truth (3 John 3),
and that the truth will live in him (2 John 3).
You are the truth, Lord (John 14:6), and "your word is truth" (John 17:17).
I pray that he will "know the truth," and the truth will set him free (John
8:32) to live in your joy forever.

**Ask God for grace to forgive any of the times your prodigal may have lied
to you. Thank Jesus for being "the way and the truth and the life" (John 14:6).**

Off Broadway

Enter through the narrow gate. For wide is the gate and broad is
the road that leads to destruction, and many enter through it. But small
is the gate and narrow the road that leads to life, and only a few find it.

MATTHEW 7:13-14

She's seen enough, Lord.
Enough entertainment to negatively impact her outlook on life
    and lead her astray from what is really living.
I pray you will loosen the grip of media on her heart and mind, Father.
Help her to be mindful of the movies she watches and the music she
    listens to.
Instead of the lyrics of popular songs filling her head,
    I pray that you will help her to hide your Word in her heart,
    that she "might not sin against you" (Psalm 119:11).
I ask that you open her eyes to the emptiness of the ways of this world.
Give her wisdom to see that those who live for this world
    are living for "what does not satisfy" (Isaiah 55:2).
Let her see the shallowness of it.
    Lift her out of self-focus and let her look to you.
Help her understand not only how those who seem to have everything live
    but also how they *die*: unhappy, unfulfilled, and separated from you.
Bring her to the place where she can genuinely ask, "What good is it for
    someone to gain the whole world, yet forfeit their soul?" (Mark 8:36).
The world around her idolizes actors and actresses and models
    and singers.

Please help her see the difference between fame and true success.

Lord Jesus, let her look to you as the example for her life.

"Whoever follows" you "will never walk in darkness,
but will have the light of life" (John 8:12).

Direct her feet from the broad way "that leads to destruction" and on to
the narrow road "that leads to life" that "only a few find."

Let her life reflect your goodness, so that she is transformed into your
"image with ever-increasing glory" (2 Corinthians 3:18).

"Whatever is right, whatever is pure, whatever is lovely, whatever is
admirable," help her to "think about such things."

Then you, "the God of peace," will be with her (Philippians 4:8–9).

I pray that she will come to understand that the real purpose of life
is not to be entertained, but to "walk with" you (Revelation 3:4).

I pray that "your name and renown" will become "the desire of our hearts,"
hers and mine, today and always (Isaiah 26:8).

———

**Pray that your prodigal will develop an inexplicable desire to be close to
God and to begin a new chapter with Him.**

Taming the Tongue

All kinds of animals, birds, reptiles and sea creatures are being tamed and have been tamed by mankind, but no human being can tame the tongue. It is a restless evil, full of deadly poison.

JAMES 3:7-8

Profanity is everywhere he turns, Lord—
    at school, at work, in so many forms of entertainment—
    and because the world finds it acceptable,
    he's been tempted to think the same way.
I pray that you would help him understand that what comes out of his
    mouth is more than just words.
"For the mouth speaks what the heart is full of" (Matthew 12:34).
Help him to see that swearing doesn't make him tough or more of a man,
    it makes him less of one.
It dishonors you and demonstrates a lack of character and self-control.
It parrots the world and shows a want of creativity.
Help him to be more careful with his words, Lord.
You've told us "that everyone will have to give account on the day
    of judgment for every empty word they have spoken" (Matthew 12:36).
I ask that you will make his conscience sensitive to every foul
    or inappropriate word that he hears.
Let him be repulsed by it, so that he loses the attraction to music or movies
    or friends that assault his ears.
Help him not to make compromises with the world. Give him grace to
    "reject every kind of evil" (1 Thessalonians 5:22).

Remind him that "a good man brings good things out of the good stored up in him, and an evil man brings evil things out of the evil stored up in him" (Matthew 12:35).

I pray he will take a stand in his own heart and mind and "fight the battle well, holding on to faith and a good conscience" (1 Timothy 1:18–19).

He can't do it on his own, Father.

Your Word says that "no human being can tame the tongue."

But you can. You can fill him with your Spirit,
if he will only let you. I pray that he will!

Then he will be able to "get rid of all moral filth and the evil that is so prevalent and humbly accept the word planted" in him, "which can save" him (James 1:21).

Then he will not be controlled by his sinful nature but by the Spirit, because the Spirit of God lives in him (see Romans 8:9 NLT).

I pray that instead of a torrent of foul words, "rivers of living water will flow from within" him (John 7:38), because he believes in you!

God told His people in Psalm 81:10, "Open wide your mouth and I will fill it." Pray your prodigal's mouth and mind and heart will be filled and inspired with the Word of God.

DAY 40

Run!

*Flee from sexual immorality. . . . Do you not know that your
bodies are temples of the Holy Spirit, who is in you, whom you
have received from God? You are not your own; you were
bought at a price. Therefore honor God with your bodies.*

1 CORINTHIANS 6:18–20

It's all around him, Lord.
On the internet, on TV, in magazines, and in the people he meets every day.
Sexual immorality reaches its poison claw out to him at every turn.
Your Word tells us that we can take our
    "stand against the devil's schemes" (Ephesians 6:11).
But when it comes to sexual immorality, you tell us to "flee"!
Father, please give him grace to see the danger and run!
Help him understand that sexual immorality threatens the health of his
    body and wages "war against" his soul (1 Peter 2:11).
Help him to "put to death . . . whatever belongs" to his "earthly nature:
    sexual immorality, impurity, lust, evil desires and greed,
    which is idolatry."
Give him grace to understand that "because of these,
    the wrath of God is coming" (Colossians 3:5–6),
    and you "will punish all those who commit such sins"
    (1 Thessalonians 4:6).
I pray that he will turn to you "with reverence and awe" (Hebrews 12:28),
    "so that the fear of God will be with" him
    to keep him "from sinning" (Exodus 20:20).

I pray that he will "learn to control" his "own body in a way that is holy and honorable" (1 Thessalonians 4:4).

Help him to turn his head, knowing "that anyone who looks at a woman lustfully has already committed adultery with her in his heart" (Matthew 5:28).

When temptation says, "Come to bed with me!" (Genesis 39:12), let him run and not look back.

Teach him the priceless value of innocence and purity, Father.

Help him take to heart that "the sexually immoral" "will not inherit the kingdom of God" (1 Corinthians 6:9).

I pray he will understand that lust is not love, and that love is a gift of your creating.

Because you invented love, I pray he will honor you with it.

Whatever mistakes he's made, please give him grace to see that your kindness leads him "to repentance" (Romans 2:4).

He can make a fresh start with you!

Cleanse his temple and fill him with your Holy Spirit (1 Corinthians 6:19).

Let there be no doubt that he belongs to you, body and soul, because you "bought" him "at a price" (1 Corinthians 6:20).

May the price of your body, given for him, give him every inspiration to give his own to you.

————

Ask God to give your prodigal a new longing for innocence in Him. Pray that any worldly ideas of sexuality will be replaced with the wisdom of God's Word and a new desire to walk closely with Him.

For Freedom from Substance Abuse

*Be careful, or your hearts will be weighed down
with carousing, drunkenness and the anxieties of life.*

LUKE 21:34

He's not being careful, Lord.

His heart is "weighed down with carousing, drunkenness
  and the anxieties of life," and he doesn't even know it.

He's given in to the world's message that he's having a good time,
  but he isn't.

He's complicated his life in ways that hurt to see.

"Who has woe? Who has sorrow? Who has strife? Who has complaints?
  Who has needless bruises? Who has bloodshot eyes?
  Those who linger over wine" (Proverbs 23:29–30).

There's been too much lingering, Lord. He likes it too much.

And "in the end it bites like a snake and poisons like a viper" (Proverbs
  23:32).

But I praise you, Father. You are the one who says "to the captives,
  'Come out,' and to those in darkness, 'Be free!'" (Isaiah 49:9).

Call him out, Lord! Out of darkness, out of dissipation, out of any alcohol
  or drug abuse, and out of relationships that contribute to these things,
  and let him find a new identity in you!

I can see him set free, Lord. Shining from head to foot, smiling and strong,
  a living example of your kindness and love.

He has "spent enough time in the past
> doing what pagans choose to do" (1 Peter 4:3).

Set him free, Father!

I know that he has to *want* to be free. So I ask you to open his eyes to see
> the consequences of his actions, and let him long for something more.

Let him "hunger and thirst for righteousness,"
> for then he "will be filled" and blessed (Matthew 5:6).

Let him "be filled with the Spirit" (Ephesians 5:18),
> because "where the Spirit of the Lord is,
> there is freedom" (2 Corinthians 3:17).

Lord Jesus, you came "to proclaim freedom for the captives and release
> from darkness for the prisoners" (Isaiah 61:1).

Help my son, Lord—he's a prisoner of his addictions.

I pray that he be "brought into the freedom and glory of the children of
> God" in every way (Romans 8:21).

I thank you that you are completely able to do this, Father.

You are able to keep him "from stumbling and to present" him before your
> "glorious presence without fault and with great joy" (Jude 24).

Let your joy be so real to him that he won't seek happiness in anything less.

I praise you in advance for the day he will tell you,
> "you have put more joy in my heart" (Psalm 4:7 ESV).

O Father, let that day be today!

————

Does your prodigal struggle with substance abuse? Imagine him or her standing strong, set free in God's love, and making new choices in the strength He gives.

DAY 42

Praise for Small Victories

Who dares despise the day of small things?

ZECHARIAH 4:10

Thank you, Father. There's progress in my daughter's life right now.
No one else may see it, but it's definitely there.
It is the work of your hand.
I praise you that this is only the beginning.
You will continue to move, and you will continue to answer prayer,
  because if we ask anything according to your will, you hear us
  (1 John 5:14).
You do not want "anyone to perish, but everyone to come
  to repentance" (2 Peter 3:9).
You want my daughter to come to you even more than I do,
  and you are drawing her to yourself.
I praise you for this "day of small things," Father (Zechariah 4:10),
  and I thank you it will turn into something much greater.
I look forward to the day my daughter will be all she can be, through your
  "incomparably great power for us who believe" (Ephesians 1:19).
That is the same power you used to raise Jesus from the dead,
  and to make me alive in Him when I was
  "dead in transgressions" (Ephesians 2:5).
If you can do it for me, you can do it for her as well!
Thank you that you are already at work.
I can *see* that now, Father, and I praise you for this small step forward
  in my daughter's life, the first of many more steps to come.

"Faith is confidence in what we hope for
      and assurance about what we do not see" (Hebrews 11:1).
Through faith I see her coming ever closer to you—forgiven,
      saved, restored, set free.
I see you using the mistakes she has made to call others "out of the
      darkness" and into your "wonderful light" (1 Peter 2:9).
I praise you for today's victory and mark it with Samuel's words:
      "Thus far the LORD has helped us" (1 Samuel 7:12).
Thank you for the days to come, in which you will help her
      even more!
My "Redeemer is strong; the LORD Almighty is his name" (Jeremiah
      50:34).
Keep moving, Lord! Thank you for hearing my prayers!
I am confident that you will carry "on to completion" the "good work"
      you have begun in her (Philippians 1:6).
Please give me grace to "fight the good fight" of faith
      until that day comes (1 Timothy 1:18 CSB).

———

**Is there a "small victory" you can celebrate in your prodigal's life today?
If so, thank God for it. If not, pray you will see one soon.**

Coming to Our Senses

When he came to his senses, he said, "How many of my father's hired servants have food to spare, and here I am starving to death!"

LUKE 15:17

Esther was worried about her son. Edwin was only three years old, the youngest of five children, and he was very sick.

The local doctor wasn't sure of the illness, but he was worried as well. He suspected leukemia. When Edwin was taken to the hospital for further testing, the results confirmed the doctor's worst fear: an aggressive form of leukemia.

It was the middle of the Great Depression and effective treatment of the disease was decades away. Blood transfusions were prescribed and Edwin's father, Jasper, was a match.

Jasper gave heroically, providing as much blood as doctors would allow. But Edwin continued to decline. Jasper and Esther hung on to hope and prayed ardently. Esther stayed close to Edwin through the night, watching and praying and caring for her little son as best she could.

Late one night, when the room was quiet, Esther heard the distinct sound of singing. She couldn't make out the words, but she later described it as the most beautiful music she had ever heard. It soothed her soul and wiped the worry from her brow. Like Jacob at Bethel, she found herself standing at "the gate of heaven" (Genesis 28:17), in the very presence of God.

The next morning she told Jasper, "Whatever happens, everything is going to be all right. I just know it. Last night, I heard angels singing."

Edwin died that day. Jasper, weakened by the frequent transfusions, contracted pneumonia and died a few months later at the age of thirty-nine. Esther was pregnant, and the son she was carrying would never know his father.

Esther never remarried, but it wasn't for lack of opportunity. She was a beautiful young woman with sparkling blue eyes.

She never became bitter. She kept her faith and the God of her faith kept her, and He cared for her every need to the end of her days. By the time I met her, her hair was white, but her eyes were still a sparkling blue. She talked to me about Jesus and made the best homemade doughnuts this side of heaven.

Esther was my maternal grandmother.

There is a strength God gives His own that is unmistakable. It cannot be rationalized or understood apart from His presence. As Pascal wrote, "the heart has its reasons, which reason does not know."[6] Sometimes *you know* that God will show himself faithful, come what may. Through faithful prayer and the touch of His Spirit, God gives the gift of "the peace of God, which transcends all understanding," that guards our hearts and our "minds in Christ Jesus" (Philippians 4:7).

That's why prayer is "the Christian's vital breath." God uses it to give us grace that we would never encounter otherwise. For the parents of prodigals, prayer is a lifeline. Just as my grandmother found supernatural strength through prayer when her son was physically dying, God will use it to impart power to parents when the souls of their children need salvation.

That lifeline moves through us to our children. God uses our prayers to reach our children wherever they may be, and to accomplish good in their lives that would not have occurred if we were not praying. Regardless of the distance, "the arm of the LORD is not too short to save, nor his ear too dull to hear" (Isaiah 59:1). The prodigal son "came to his senses" in a far country (Luke 15:17).

---

6. Pascal, *Pensees*, 4. 277, available at ccel.org/ccel/pascal/pensees.v.html.

The parents of prodigals may "come to their senses" as well, especially where prayer is concerned. God frequently moves through our challenging circumstances to cause us to pray more than we ever have before. He uses our prayers to pull us close and show us what He alone can do. He sharpens our "spiritual senses," giving us the peace that we so desperately need and a fresh strength that we never knew was possible.

We may even hear angels sing.

Jesus said, "there is rejoicing in the presence of the angels of God over one sinner who repents" (Luke 15:10). And in His presence, there is all the help that we need.

Prayer is the Christian's vital breath,
the Christian's native air.
His watchword at the gates of death;
he enters heaven with prayer.

—JAMES MONTGOMERY,
"PRAYER IS THE SOUL'S SINCERE DESIRE"

When You've Said Something You Regret

Set a guard over my mouth, LORD;
keep watch over the door of my lips.

PSALM 141:3

I did it again, Lord. I spoke to my child in anger,
    and it wasn't the right response.
I know there are times when I'm permitted to be angry at the wrong in her
    life, but your Word also says, "tremble and do not sin" (Psalm 4:4).
I went too far and said things I should not have said.
Forgive me, Lord, and give me fresh grace.
Because you give "grace to the humble" (Proverbs 3:34 CSB),
    I humble myself before you and ask you to show me
    "the most excellent way" (1 Corinthians 12:31).
I know that "if I speak in the tongues of men or of angels, but do not
    have love, I am only a resounding gong or a clanging cymbal"
    (1 Corinthians 13:1).
I also know that "human anger does not produce the righteousness that
    God desires" (James 1:20).
So I ask you to help me to do the hard thing and ask for my child's forgiveness.
I pray that you will give her grace to accept my apology
    so that our relationship can be healed.
I really want to "do everything in love," Father (1 Corinthians 16:14),
    but right now I find parenting so difficult.

I need you to take up "my case" and "uphold my cause" (Lamentations
    3:58–59) so that she will see you at work even in this situation.
You are the one "who daily bears our burdens" (Psalm 68:19),
    and I ask you to carry me through this and give me wisdom.
I thank you that you can take even actions with imperfect motives
    and use them "for good" and "the saving of many lives"
    (Genesis 50:20).
"Set a guard over my mouth, LORD" (Psalm 141:3)
    so that "the fruit of that righteousness will be peace" (Isaiah 32:17).
May the word of Christ dwell in me richly so that I may "teach and
    admonish" "with all wisdom" (Colossians 3:16).
You, "speaking in righteousness," are "mighty to save" (Isaiah 63:1 ESV).
Whisper your truth to my daughter's heart, Lord, and save her!
You are "able to save completely" those who come to you (Hebrews 7:25).
Let her come to you, Lord!
You said, "I have loved you with an everlasting love;
    I have drawn you with unfailing kindness" (Jeremiah 31:3).
Draw her with love, Father!
I love you because you loved me first (1 John 4:19).
Please do the same for my child.
"May these words of my mouth and this meditation of my heart be
    pleasing in your sight" (Psalm 19:14) so that her joy "in Christ Jesus
    will abound on account of me" (Philippians 1:26).

———

Scripture tells us that "no human being can tame the tongue," calling it "a restless evil" (James 3:8). But it also says "let the word of Christ dwell in you richly" (Colossians 3:16 ESV). Ask God to replace any bitterness in your words or thoughts toward your prodigal with our Savior's encouragement and love.

Manipulated

You intended to harm me, but God intended it for good to accomplish what is now being done, the saving of many lives.

GENESIS 50:20

Here we go again, Lord.

I've been manipulated once again.

I want to believe the best things about my child,

    but sometimes he takes advantage of that!

He wants me to trust him, and I want to be able to!

And then something happens that makes trust difficult.

But it's not just my son who is doing the manipulating, Father.

He's being manipulated by the Adversary, and he doesn't even know it.

He's being conformed to "the pattern of this world" when he needs to

    be transformed by the renewing of his mind (Romans 12:2).

He's being deceived (Genesis 3:13), and my heart aches for him.

But this battle for his heart and his mind is not over.

"The battle is the LORD's" (1 Samuel 17:47).

"Strength and wisdom are his;

    deceivers and deceived are both in his power" (Job 12:16 NLT).

I have already given my son to you, Father, and I give him to

    you again.

Just like you prayed for Peter, Lord Jesus, when the devil went after him,

    I pray that my son's "faith may not fail" (Luke 22:31–32).

"Spirit of truth," I ask that you guide him "into all the truth" (John 16:13)

    so that he will "overcome the evil one" (1 John 2:13).

Father, although my son has been deceived, I pray that you will use
even this circumstance "for good" and "the saving of many lives"!
When he turns, let him turn others to you.
Then "no weapon forged against" us will prevail (Isaiah 54:17).
I look forward to the day when I will be able to look my son in the eye
and know that he is telling the truth,
because he is "walking in the truth" (2 John 4).
What a joy that will be!
I praise you in advance for the day my son's faith will be restored,
when he will shout to you with gratitude,
"You have become my salvation" (Psalm 118:21)!
"Hallelujah! Salvation and glory and power belong to our God"
(Revelation 19:1).
The victory will be yours, and the blessing will be ours!
Amen.

———

Have you been manipulated by your prodigal? Ask God to help you completely forgive, and ask Him for fresh wisdom. He promises to give wisdom "generously" (James 1:5) when we ask!

Songs in the Night

By day the LORD directs his love, at night his song is with me—
a prayer to the God of my life.

PSALM 42:8

I can't sleep, Lord, and you know why.
I'm worried about my child.
I know you told me not to worry about *my* life (Matthew 6:25),
    but is it okay if I talk to you about hers?
I remember when she was just a baby, and things were so much easier.
Thank you for those days. They were a gift!
But you know the situation we're in now, Father.
I never saw this coming. Not like this.
    Do any parents think their child will go through prodigal years?
I always thought things like this happen to *other* people,
    and I have to admit I've sometimes been too quick
    to come up with a reason *why.*
It's easier to parent someone else's kids in our own minds
    without knowing what those parents are really going through, isn't it?
My daughter and I are up against it tonight, Lord, and we need you so much.
I need the peace "which transcends all understanding"
    to guard my heart and mind in you (Philippians 4:7).
She needs your light to shine on her path and lead her
    "from darkness to light" (Acts 26:18).
You are "the light of the world," Lord Jesus (John 8:12).
    And you are my light tonight.

You are "God my Maker, who gives songs in the night" (Job 35:10).
I stand on the promise of your Word tonight:

"Indeed, God is my salvation; I will trust him and not be afraid,
For the LORD, the LORD himself, is my strength and my song.
He has become my salvation" (Isaiah 12:2 CSB).
Thank you that when I "do not know what to do" (2 Chronicles 20:12),

I can look to you for the direction I need.
You are "the way and the truth and the life" (John 14:6).
"With you is the fountain of life; in your light we see light" (Psalm 36:9).
I place this situation in your hands, Lord, and cast on you

every worry, every need, every care (Psalm 55:22).
You said, "Come to me, all you who are weary and burdened,

and I will give you rest" (Matthew 11:28).
That describes me pretty well right now, so I come.
And I bring my child with me in the arms of faith and prayer.
I praise you because your "light shines in the darkness,"

and the darkness will not overcome it (John 1:5).
"In peace I will lie down and sleep" (Psalm 4:8),

because you are my hope.
The future looks bright with you!

———

Ask the Lord to give you a moment's rest from your worries. Read Psalm 23, and imagine yourself as His sheep, resting with Him in a peaceful place.

Accepting Rejection

He was despised and rejected by mankind, a man of suffering,
and familiar with pain. Like one from whom people hide
their faces he was despised, and we held him in low esteem.

ISAIAH 53:3

Father, right now my child doesn't understand that if I really love her,
  I'm not going to let her do whatever she wants.
She's angry with me about that, and we need your help.
I pray that in her anger, she will not sin and choose to do
  what I've told her she cannot.
I pray that the devil will not gain a foothold in this (Ephesians 4:26–27).
I ask instead that your peace will rule in her heart (Colossians 3:15).
I also ask that you will protect her from friends
  who would lead her "astray" (Proverbs 12:26).
Father, I pray that you would not allow the "bitter root" of defiance
  to take hold in any way (Hebrews 12:15).
Instead, "let salvation spring up, let righteousness flourish with it"
  (Isaiah 45:8).
I pray that she will mature through this
  and "reject the wrong and choose the right" (Isaiah 7:16).
I ask that you would quietly speak to her and teach her "your way, LORD"
  so that she will "rely on your faithfulness"
  with an "undivided heart" (Psalm 86:11).
Help her to understand not only how much I love her, but most of all,
  how much you do.

You know what it's like to have those you love reject you,
  because you came to earth, and we "did not receive" you (John 1:11).
You chose to accept our rejection for our own benefit, to save us and
  set us free.
In a small way I'm beginning to understand some of that, Lord.
It's *because* I love her that I'm trying to help her to choose what is right,
  despite her defiance.
Thank you, Father, for doing that for us.
Your Word makes this so very clear:
Even when we were your "enemies," you chose to reconcile us
  "through the death" of your son (Romans 5:10).
"This is love: not that we loved God, but that he loved us and sent his
  Son as an atoning sacrifice for our sins" (1 John 4:10).
Dear Jesus, I commit my daughter to you afresh.
Rescue her from this world, Lord, and keep her from the mistake
  of choosing her way over your own.
Your Word says, "Whoever turns a sinner from the error of their way will
  save them from death and cover over a multitude of sins" (James 5:20).
Thank you for saving me. Save her too, I pray!

———

It's hard when others reject us, especially those we love. Thank Jesus that
He understands what it's like to be rejected, and praise Him for His promise
that "whoever comes to me I will never drive away" (John 6:37).

When Distance Separates

Surely the arm of the LORD is not too short to save,
nor his ear too dull to hear.

ISAIAH 59:1

Father, I thank you there is nowhere my son can go
  where you are not already present.
Even though he is far from me,
  I rest in the promise that your arm "is not too short to save."
I pray that you will meet him where he is, Lord.
Let him encounter you everywhere he turns, "behind and before"
  (Psalm 139:5).
Open his eyes to "paths of life" that lead in your direction
  and draw him close to you (Acts 2:28).
Father, he needs you to point him home.
Not home to me, but to his eternal home with you.
Just like the prodigal son who "came to his senses" in a far country,
  I ask that he will become aware of anything that separates him
  from you.
May he say, "I will set out and go back to my father"
  and run to your open arms (Luke 15:17–18).
Even where he is now, he is not so far away that your love cannot reach
  him, because "the earth is filled with your love, LORD" (Psalm 119:64).
Let your love surround him and keep him from all harm.
Father, give him "more grace" to submit himself to you and
  "resist the devil," so the devil "will flee" from him (James 4:6–7).

Fill his heart with faith, because then he will be helped in every way and
"shielded" by your power (1 Peter 1:5).
Send your angels to help him, as you do for those who "inherit salvation"
(Hebrews 1:14).
I pray you will bring him new friends who know you,
and keep him from those who would lead him astray.
Give him a longing to be part of "the family of believers" (Galatians 6:10),
where he will be encouraged, helped, and blessed.
Let every road that he takes lead to you, Lord.
Thank you, Father, that you hear my prayer.
Thank you that you are even more willing to answer than I am to ask.
I praise you that you are "able to do immeasurably more than all
we ask or imagine" (Ephesians 3:20).
I praise you for the ways you will answer this prayer!

Being separated from those we love can be difficult, especially when we don't know what is happening in their lives. Thank God that there's nowhere your prodigal can run where His love and power (or your prayers) cannot reach.

Praise in the Dark

About midnight Paul and Silas were praying and singing
hymns to God, and the other prisoners were listening to them.

ACTS 16:25

What Paul and Silas did was beautiful and inspiring, Father.

Even though they had been "stripped" and "severely flogged" and were
in a dark jail cell after midnight with their feet in stocks, they were
praising you (Acts 16:22–24).

What an amazing example! Please give me grace to do the same when
I feel defeated and in the dark.

I want to give you the glory due your name (1 Chronicles 16:29)
and continue praising you even when I don't know what the
next day brings.

You are always worthy of praise.

When I don't feel like drawing near to you, that's when I need to praise
you most of all, because you "strengthen the feeble hands"
and "steady the knees that give way."

You "say to those with fearful hearts, 'Be strong, do not fear;
your God will come'" (Isaiah 35:3–4).

When it's the middle of the night and I'm wondering if my child
is safe, I will find "courage to pray to you" (1 Chronicles 17:25).

Just as David "found strength in the LORD his God" when his family was
in danger (1 Samuel 30:6), I know you can give me grace to persevere.

"My heart says of you, 'Seek his face!'
Your face, LORD, I will seek" (Psalm 27:8).

I pray for grace to seek "your face with all my heart" (Psalm 119:58).

When I'm wondering why things have happened even though I have been trying to parent my child as well as I can, I will "not rely on" myself "but on" you (2 Corinthians 1:9).

When it feels like my prayers are bouncing off the ceiling and going no farther, I thank you that my faith is not dependent upon feelings.

I praise you, Lord Jesus, that even when our faith is weak you will "[remain] faithful" (2 Timothy 2:13).

I've never been through anything like what happened to Paul and Silas, but if you gave them strength to praise you then, and you are "the same yesterday and today and forever" (Hebrews 13:8), then you can do the same for me.

Together, we will win "the victory" in my child's life (1 John 5:4).

May she see your Spirit in me, and may it draw her to you.

Then we will praise you together, our Savior and our God!

———

Are you having difficulty seeing answers to prayer in your prodigal's life? Intentionally praise God (see Hebrews 13:15) despite your circumstances, anticipating His faithfulness and love.

DAY 49

Constant Help

God is our refuge and strength, an ever-present help in trouble.

PSALM 46:1

Father, you're not just an occasional help when times are tough.

I praise you because you're an "ever-present help"!

There is never a day, an hour, a minute, or a moment when you are
not attentive.

You are truly amazing, God! You "neither slumber nor sleep" (Psalm 121:4).

Nothing gets past you. Not a "careless word" (Matthew 12:36 ESV)
or the slightest "inclination of" our thoughts (Genesis 6:5).

Even the hairs of our heads "are all numbered" (Luke 12:7).

Because you are my "help and shield," I will trust in you (Psalm 115:11).

Because your name is a "fortified tower,"

I'm going to keep running to you (Proverbs 18:10), my faithful Savior!

You give me the strength to go on (Psalm 29:11).

You know why I'm here, Lord. I'm here to ask for your mercy
and intervention.

I know that apart from you, I can do nothing (John 15:5).

I come to you for my child again, and I'm going to keep coming as long as
you give me "breath" (Isaiah 42:5).

Isn't that what your Word says?

"You who call on the LORD, give yourselves no rest" (Isaiah 62:6–7).

You want me to keep coming to you for my child again and again.

You want me to "pray continually" (1 Thessalonians 5:17).

So I make this prayer my *declaration of dependence* on you.

You know how my child will return to you. You know the day
and the hour. You know exactly what it will take.
Thank you, Father, that you never tire of hearing my prayers
for my child.
Thank you, Lord Jesus, that you are able to save my son "completely,"
and that you go to the Father for us every day (Hebrews 7:25).
Thank you, Holy Spirit, that when I don't know exactly what to pray,
you intercede for me "with groanings that cannot be expressed
in words" (Romans 8:26 NLT).
I will "approach God's throne of grace with confidence, so that we may
receive mercy and find grace to help us in our time of need"
(Hebrews 4:16).
I will come to you for him again and again, like the mother
who kept crying out to you for her daughter (Matthew 15:23),
and the father who begged you to look at his son (Luke 9:38).
Until my son runs to you, and you take him in your arms and bless him,
I will keep praying, day after day.
And then I'll pray again, thanking you with all my heart, "proclaiming
aloud your praise and telling of all your wonderful deeds"
(Psalm 26:7).

———

**Thank the Lord that He never tires of your asking for help for your prodigal.
He loves it when you come to Him!**

Treasured in Our Hearts

Then he went down to Nazareth with them and was obedient to them.
But his mother treasured all these things in her heart.

LUKE 2:51

When Jesus was a boy, Mary and Joseph left him behind in Jerusalem without knowing it. He was "in the temple courts" when they found him, "sitting among the teachers, listening to them and asking them questions" (Luke 2:46). Mary asked for an explanation, and Jesus answered, "Why were you searching for me? . . . Didn't you know I had to be in my Father's house?" (Luke 2:49).

She wasn't sure what he meant at the time. But she did know something was happening. Something beautiful. Something good. God was at work, and Mary understood that. So she "treasured all these things in her heart" (Luke 2:51).

I have some treasures too. Treasured memories from the Father's house when Katie was little. Bright eyes on sunny Sundays, taking it all in: "Look what I made you, Daddy!" A crayon card from Sunday school. Cuddling as close as she could when she sat beside me in worship. Simple prayers offered with a child's soaring faith. A little, lilting voice singing sweetly: "Jesus loves me, this I know . . ."

Jesus loved my little girl, and she knew it. Her childlike faith was simple and sincere, a gift from heaven untainted by the world. Like Mary, I could see that something was happening. God was at work in her little life. And that continues to give me hope.

Today's difficult days won't last forever. God is faithful. The seeds that grew and bloomed in the springtime of my daughter's life will one day flower again.

This is more than wishful thinking. The promises in God's Word give me hope. Promises like "From everlasting to everlasting the LORD's love is with those who fear him, and his righteousness with their children's children" (Psalm 103:17), and "For the LORD is good and his love endures forever; his faithfulness continues through all generations" (Psalm 100:5).

I am resolved to pray for my daughter every day, and I take comfort in the fact that God looks forward to the day she returns to her faith even more than I.

G. K. Chesterton wrote that "we have sinned and grown old, and our Father is younger than we."[7] God abounds with life. Though He was "before all ages" (Jude 25), He knows no age. His strength is unfathomable: "The LORD is the everlasting God, the Creator of the ends of the earth. He will not grow tired or weary" (Isaiah 40:28). The seemingly limitless energy children have is just a pale reflection of His infinite, unfailing strength.

His amazing strength is able to pursue my daughter long after my own is gone. Because of His faithfulness, the prayers I've placed before the Father's throne will still be there, waiting to be answered in His perfect wisdom and way. E. M. Bounds, a minister and chaplain during the Civil War, understood this: "God shapes the world by prayer. Prayers are deathless. The lips that uttered them may be closed in death, the heart that felt them may have ceased to beat, but the prayers live before God, and God's heart is set on them. Prayers outlive the lives of those who uttered them; outlive a generation, outlive an age, outlive a world."[8]

"God's heart is set on them." He will receive the prayers offered in faith with an everlasting love that "never fails" (1 Corinthians 13:8).

---

7. Chesterton, *Orthodoxy*, 60.
8. Bounds, *Complete Works*, 299.

So I will run to Him for her. I will pour out my heart in prayer, knowing that He is completely in agreement that she needs to turn her heart to Him. I will carry her to Him in the arms of prayer, because I still treasure her in my heart, and I always will.

As much as I treasure her, He treasures her more. If her childhood faith is precious to me, the worth of it to Him is incalculable.

So here she is, Father, our treasured child: yours, mine, ours.

I bring her to you once again.

Your prayers, dear child of God . . . shall be answered—
some of them, perhaps, during your lifetime on earth,
and all of them, certainly, during your lifetime in heaven.

— SAMUEL PRIME

When She Hasn't Come Home Yet

I am like a desert owl, like an owl among the ruins.
I lie awake; I have become like a bird alone on a roof.

PSALM 102:6-7

It's been one of those nights, Lord.

She should have been home hours ago.

So I sit here, waiting.

Waiting for the phone to ring.

Waiting for the sound of the car in the driveway
    and her footsteps on the front porch.

Be with her, Lord. You know where she is.

Please watch over her, Father, and keep her safe.

I thank you that you are still in control,
    regardless of the choices my child makes.

"How great you are, Sovereign LORD!

There is no one like you, and there is no God but you" (2 Samuel 7:22).

"Even the darkness will not be dark to you; the night will shine
    like the day, for darkness is as light to you" (Psalm 139:12).

Even at this moment, turn her thoughts home.

Not just to me, but to you.

I want her to call home, but most of all I want her to call on your name.

"You, Lord, are forgiving and good,
    abounding in love to all who call to you" (Psalm 86:5).

"The Lord is near to all who call on him,
  to all who call on him in truth" (Psalm 145:18).
You richly bless all who call on you (Romans 10:12),
    because "everyone who calls on the name of the Lord will be saved"
    (Acts 2:21).
Please bring her home, Father. All the way home.
Let her heart be at home in your presence,
    because that's what she needs most of all.
I want her to obey me, Lord Jesus, but even more I want her
    to obey *you*.
You said, "Anyone who loves me will obey my teaching.
    My Father will love them, and we will come to them
    and make our home with them" (John 14:23).
Your Word also says, "The children of your servants will live in
    your presence; their descendants will be established before you"
    (Psalm 102:28). Oh, how I want her to live with you and for you!
I'm holding on to that promise tighter than ever tonight, Lord,
    so please hold on to *her*, just as you said you would.
Take her by the hand.
Take her by the heart.
And lead her *home*.

––––––––––

Take comfort in the fact that when you don't know where your prodigal is, God still does. Pray for the Lord's safe keeping for your prodigal and His peace for you.

Light His Feet

Your word is a lamp for my feet, a light on my path.

PSALM 119:105

Your Word is amazing, Father!

It has the power to transform lives.

It is "alive and active. Sharper than any double-edged sword,

it penetrates even to dividing soul and spirit, joints and marrow;

it judges the thoughts and attitudes of the heart" (Hebrews 4:12–13).

How I love your Word!

I pray that you will release the power of your Word into my son's life.

Let your light fall on his feet and on his path.

So many people are telling him where to turn and what to do.

He needs to hear your voice, Lord.

"How can a young person stay on the path of purity?

By living according to your word" (Psalm 119:9).

I pray that you will direct his "footsteps according to your word"

and "let no sin rule over" him (Psalm 119:133).

Only you can lead him "along the right paths"

and restore his soul (Psalm 23:3).

He has a Bible. I pray that he will pick it up and read it!

Let him meet you in it, Father, and hear your voice in a way that he

hasn't in a long time, because "you yourself" are teaching him

(Psalm 119:102).

I pray you will open his eyes so that he "may see wonderful things"

in your Word (Psalm 119:18).

Your Word is able to make him "wise for salvation through faith
in Christ Jesus" (2 Timothy 3:15).

Bring his heart back to you as he reads so that there is no doubt
about his relationship with you.

Give him a hunger for your Word—fill his heart and mind with it.

Let him turn to it every day, because "man shall not live on bread alone,
but on every word that comes from" you (Matthew 4:4).

As he spends time in your Word, let him see how you are speaking
to him about the intimate details of his life.

Then as a "servant of God," "thoroughly equipped for every good work"
(2 Timothy 3:17), let him "speak your word with great boldness"
(Acts 4:29) so that others may hear it and love it too!

––––––

Jesus reminded us that we do not live "on bread alone, but on every word
that comes from the mouth of God" (Matthew 4:4). Pray that your prodigal
will hunger deeply for God's Word and truth.

Shame Off Her!

As Scripture says, "Anyone who believes in him
will never be put to shame."

ROMANS 10:11

I can see my daughter standing before you, dressed in white.

It's her wedding day! But not on this earth.

There she is, in the kingdom of God, where your church is "prepared as a
bride beautifully dressed for her husband" (Revelation 21:2).

I pray that day will come for her, Lord Jesus!

That day in which she knows with all of her heart that whoever trusts in
you "will never be put to shame."

She trusted in you once, Lord, and I believe that you "began
a good work" in her and will "carry it on to completion"
(Philippians 1:6).

I pray you will move soon in her life to turn her heart from sin
back to you.

Let her hear your Spirit speaking to her: "I have swept away your
offenses like a cloud, your sins like the morning mist.
Return to me, for I have redeemed you" (Isaiah 44:22).

Let the fog clear and a bright new morning break!

Even when we rebel against you, you long for us to give our hearts
to you.

When we do, you take our sins completely away.

You clothe us with "garments of salvation"
and "a robe of . . . righteousness" (Isaiah 61:10).

You present us holy in your sight,

"without blemish and free from accusation" (Colossians 1:22).

You have said, "You will forget the shame of your youth" (Isaiah 54:4).

And you choose to forget it as well!

You tell us you will remember our sins no more (Jeremiah 31:34).

Take the shame off my daughter, Lord Jesus! Just as you have for me.

You promise in your Word, "Do not be afraid; you will not be put to shame.

Do not fear disgrace; you will not be humiliated" (Isaiah 54:4).

I pray my daughter will understand that when prodigals return,

you throw a party!

You welcome them with open arms!

Let her know deeply in her heart that there is no shame in being

your child.

Let her know that any name she has been called doesn't matter,

because one day, you will give a "new name" to all you have saved

(Revelation 3:12), all who live for your kingdom and your love.

May any sin or shame from the past be washed away

by your "precious blood" (1 Peter 1:19).

May she live so in love with you that others are drawn to you as well!

I know she has a choice to make, and I pray she will make it soon and

"choose life" (Deuteronomy 30:19).

I pray she will choose you!

———

Pray that your prodigal will feel "godly sorrow" which "brings repentance" (2 Corinthians 7:10), and he or she will come to know the joy of forgiveness through Jesus.

What the Locusts Have Eaten

I will repay you for the years the locusts have eaten.

JOEL 2:25

"I will repay you for the years the locusts have eaten."

I love that promise, Lord. It shows me the kindness of your heart.

I praise you that there is no hurt that you cannot heal, no loss you cannot restore.

You make "everything new" (Revelation 21:5).

I look forward to the day you will make everything new in my child's life.

You have a bright future waiting for her!

I pray she will open her heart to you and receive your mercy.

I thank you that even "the years the locusts have eaten" can be turned to blessing, and I ask you to do that!

You are so resourceful, Father. You can use anything!

There is not a step my child has taken that cannot be one day turned toward you.

You came to "those living in darkness and in the shadow of death, to guide our feet into the path of peace" (Luke 1:79).

You tell the story, Jesus, of leaving ninety-nine sheep to go after the one that is lost.

How wonderful you are to go after "lost sheep"!

When you find the lost one, you "rejoice" (Luke 15:4–6).

I ask that the damage the adversary has tried to cause in my child's life will be completely undone so that *she will praise you,* just as you long for her to do.

Your Word says, from the lips of "children and infants" you have ordained
praise "to silence the foe and the avenger" (Psalm 8:2).

I praise you too, Father.

I praise you because you love her with infinite love.

I long for my child to come home to you.

You long for that too, even more than I do, because you are "not wanting
anyone to perish, but everyone to come to repentance" (2 Peter 3:9).

May she come to you *today*, Lord!

Let her heart be touched by your kindness
and her mind opened to the wonder of who you are.

Let her hear you say, "I am with you and will rescue you" (Jeremiah 1:8).

Let her answer when you call and come running with a repenting heart,
drawn by the hope you alone can give.

You have said, "those who hope in me will not be disappointed"
(Isaiah 49:23). And she won't be!

You are my hope, Lord, and I pray that you soon will be hers.

"You are God my Savior, and my hope is in you all day long" (Psalm 25:5).

Even though she doesn't know it now, I thank you that she will
one day "know the hope" to which you have called her
(Ephesians 1:18), and praise you for it with all of her heart.

**Thank God that He is able to replace difficult years in your prodigal's life
with good. Praise Him that He can use anything—even bad choices—to
draw your prodigal near.**

Straight Steps

*Trust in the L*ORD *with all your heart*
and do not lean on your own understanding.
In all your ways acknowledge him,
and he will make straight your paths.

PROVERBS 3:5–6 ESV

Sometimes I don't understand the choices my child makes, Lord.
He doesn't seem able to see the consequences of some actions
     and the pointlessness of others. Or he doesn't care.
He needs a breakthrough, Father. I ask that you lead him to one.
You are the "One who breaks open the way" (Micah 2:13).
You promise in your Word, "I instruct you in the way of wisdom
     and lead you along straight paths" (Proverbs 4:11).
I pray that promise for him today.
More than anything else, he needs to acknowledge you and trust you,
     because "the fear of the LORD is the beginning of wisdom"
     (Psalm 111:10).
I ask that you help him to think about eternity.
Help him to see that there is so much more to life
     than simply living for the moment.
Let him understand that the road he's on doesn't lead him to
     where he wants to be.
"Wide is the gate and broad is the road that leads to destruction,
     and many enter through it" (Matthew 7:13).
Let him turn from that road, Father!

I ask that you will give him grace to be "a wise son, endowed with intelligence and discernment" (2 Chronicles 2:12).

Make him an "upright" man, who "[gives] thought to" his "ways" (Proverbs 21:29).

Place wise people in his path who he will listen to.

I ask that you will enable me to communicate with him so that he will listen, and that you will speak to him through me.

Your Word tells us to "get wisdom, get understanding" (Proverbs 4:5).

It also says, "Blessed are those who find wisdom . . . for she [wisdom] is more profitable than silver and yields better returns than gold" (Proverbs 3:13–14).

I want good things for my son, Father.

But most of all, I want what you can give him.

Your Word says that "to the person who pleases him, God gives wisdom, knowledge and happiness" (Ecclesiastes 2:26).

You are all of these things, Father, and so much more!

I ask that you make his steps straight so that they lead him straight to you!

———

Walk as you pray, and pray that every step your prodigal takes will lead him or her closer to Jesus.

Of God's Choosing

*When I came to the spring today, I said, "Lᴏʀᴅ,
God of my master Abraham, if you will, please grant
success to the journey on which I have come."*

GENESIS 24:42

The way you answered Abraham's servant's prayer
    for a wife for Isaac is beautiful, Father.
He was looking for your direction and blessing, and you gave it
    to him.
I'd like to ask the same thing for my child, Lord.
You know exactly the right person to make the ideal spouse for her—not
    just for earthly reasons, but for heavenly ones.
I ask for someone of your choosing.
I pray that you will lead my daughter to a man
    who will be a blessing to her soul.
Wherever he is right now,
    I ask that you bless him and prepare them both for one another.
I pray that he will be part of your purpose in calling her to yourself,
    a man who loves you and "is known by" you (1 Corinthians 8:3).
I ask that even now you will move in his heart and mind to equip him
    "with everything good" for doing your will, and that you would
    work in him "what is pleasing" to you (Hebrews 13:21).
Let her see you at work in him and be drawn to you all the more
    because of it.
Lord Jesus, let him love my daughter with a sacrificial love

that you alone can give, just as you loved the church
and gave yourself up for her (Ephesians 5:25).

I pray that love will be much more than simply a feeling for both
of them.

I ask that your "perfect love" (1 John 4:18) will be at work in them
so that they will both honor you above themselves,
and their marriage will stand the test of time.

I pray that he will "enjoy life" with the wife he loves (Ecclesiastes 9:9),
and that your peace will rest upon the home they make together.

Bring them to the place where they can say together with all of their hearts,
"As for me and my household, we will serve the LORD" (Joshua 24:15).

Let him "rejoice in the wife of" his youth (Proverbs 5:18),
and let her be a source of blessing and joy to him.

Let them worship you "with gladness" (Psalm 100:2) for the gift
of each other, and "praise you in the presence of your faithful people"
(Psalm 52:9).

Father, I'd also like to ask you that you bless them with children
who will walk with you so that "from generation to generation
we will proclaim your praise" (Psalm 79:13).

I praise you in this moment for your kindness and faithfulness to answer
this prayer, not only today, but in the years to come!

As you pray take both hands and place them over your heart. Pray that God will bless your prodigal with a friend who deeply loves the Lord.

Inexhaustible

Even youths grow tired and weary,
and young men stumble and fall;
but those who hope in the LORD
will renew their strength.
They will soar on wings like eagles;
they will run and not grow weary,
they will walk and not be faint.

ISAIAH 40:30–31

Someday she'll get tired, Lord.

Tired of this world and its false promises.

Tired of running from you.

On that day I pray that she will discover the strength that only you
can give.

Right now her energy seems boundless. But it won't last forever.

"Even youths grow tired and weary, and young men stumble and fall."

If she must stumble, I pray it will be into your arms.

If she must fall, I pray it will be in love with you.

Then she will find strength that she never knew was possible!

I praise you for the strength you give, Father.

You give "strength to the weary,"

and increase "the power of the weak" (Isaiah 40:29).

With you dwelling inside of her heart, she will have a source of energy
brighter than the sun, unlimited, infinite, eternal!

That's what you are, Father! Nothing compares to you!

I pray that she will find in you her "inexhaustible treasure . . . where
no thief comes near and no moth destroys" (Luke 12:33 CSB).

Then, even when her body ages and her strength fails, she will not
"lose heart."

"Though outwardly we are wasting away, yet inwardly we are being
renewed day by day" by your inexhaustible mercy and love
(2 Corinthians 4:16).

I pray that she will run to you "and not grow weary."

I pray she will not only run, but soar!

Let her heart and mind take flight with the wonder of all that you are.

Let her humble herself under your "mighty hand,"
that you may lift her up (1 Peter 5:6).

Lifted in your hands, she *will* rise!

I pray she can "be strong and courageous," because you go with her,
and you "will never leave" her "nor forsake" her (Deuteronomy 31:6).

Then she will hear you say, "you who lie in the dust,
awake and shout for joy" (Isaiah 26:19 NASB).

Then together we *will* shout for joy!

And we will sing your praise for all eternity!

**Praise the Lord for being the Good Shepherd who pursues us with love, no
matter how lost or far away we may be.**

Waiting for an Answer

Jesus did not answer a word. So his disciples came to him and urged him, "Send her away, for she keeps crying out after us."

MATTHEW 15:23

When our daughter was fifteen she ran away.

Katie had fallen in with the wrong crowd at school. When we grounded her and pulled her out of school to finish the final weeks of her sophomore year at home, she made other plans. One day she ran out the door and down the street, where a friend picked her up in a car.

She was gone more than three weeks.

Those were the longest three weeks of our lives. Cari and I looked everywhere for our daughter and sought help from law enforcement and friends. But no matter how hard we tried, it seemed like we were always a few steps behind her.

Her life was in danger, and she didn't even know it. One day, Cari and I found ourselves sitting in the apartment of an armed drug dealer who knew some of Katie's friends and had seen her recently. Later, we discovered she was even a passenger in a wreck where the car rolled and others were injured. She left the scene when the police arrived.

In the desperate days that followed, Cari and I learned the importance of waiting on God in prayer for those we love.[9] We had no other choice.

---

9. Additional details of this lesson learned about prayer are shared in the author's book *The Lost Art of Praying Together*, chapter 6.

We had come to the end of our strength and resources and *had* to rely on God. The more we prayed, the more effective our search became.

It was on a Father's Day that we found her. Cari and I were in a restaurant parking lot, on our way to dinner, when the phone rang. A waitress at another restaurant had spotted her. Katie was only three blocks away. We soon had her home, safe and sound.

God always answers prayer. The answer is either *yes, no,* or *wait*. When the answer is *wait*, it's easy to confuse it with no answer at all.

One of the more challenging stories from the Bible is Jesus's encounter with a Canaanite woman who "came to him, crying out, 'Lord, Son of David, have mercy on me! My daughter is demon-possessed and suffering terribly.'"

The challenging part comes in the next verse: "Jesus did not answer a word" (Matthew 15:22–23).

Why? Didn't Jesus care about the woman and her daughter? Hadn't He come to "destroy the devil's work" (1 John 3:8)? What was Jesus doing?

Jesus's silence speaks volumes. We *have to wait* on God when we pray. We may not know how He will answer, but we do know He is pleased when we pursue Him and put our hearts before Him constantly in prayer.

The Canaanite woman persisted with Jesus. When he told her, "I was sent only to the lost sheep of Israel," she "came and knelt before him" and asked again. When He responded, "It is not right to take the children's bread and toss it to their dogs," that still didn't stop her.

"'Yes, Lord,' she said, 'but even the dogs eat the crumbs that fall from their masters' table.'"

Then came the answer she was longing to hear: "Woman, you have great faith! Your request is granted" (Matthew 15:24–28).

It took some time to get there. But she persisted because she loved her daughter and knew she was asking for something good for her.

The same is true when we pray for our prodigal kids. Sometimes the answers don't come when we would hope. Things may even seem to go from bad to worse. But we have to persevere, keep believing, and keep asking.

Like the Canaanite woman, we know we are asking for a good thing when we pray for God to change our children's hearts. We have the assurance that Jesus loves our children, because He died to make their salvation possible. When we ask Him to save them, we know we're praying for the very thing He wants to do.

Waiting is never easy, but the end result is worth it. David put it this way: "Those who know your name will trust in you, for you, LORD, have never forsaken those who seek you" (Psalm 9:10).

Keep seeking! Keep trusting! Keep asking! Keep praying!

There is grace to be found in the waiting, even if it takes years for the answer to come.

God's silence is never "the final word."

We must wait for God, long, meekly, in the wind and wet,
in the thunder and lightning, in the cold and the dark. Wait,
and he will come. He never comes to those who do not wait.

—FREDERICK W. FABER

A Discerning Heart

Those who are wise will shine like the brightness of the heavens,
and those who lead many to righteousness, like the stars for ever and ever.

DANIEL 12:3

Father, I love what Solomon asked of you when he was a very
young man: "give your servant a discerning heart . . . to distinguish
between right and wrong" (1 Kings 3:9).
My son needs to distinguish between right and wrong, Father,
and I also need wisdom as I try to help him.
I pray that you will give a discerning heart to both of us.
I ask for your wisdom to parent this child, Father,
and to discover all the right ways to point him to you.
My wisdom is so limited, Father. I can't do this without your help.
And I thank you that I have it!
I thank you for your promise that "if any of you lacks wisdom,
he should ask God, who gives generously to all
without finding fault" (James 1:5).
I praise you because you don't find fault, Father!
I ask for the discernment you alone can give, because "the wisdom of this
world is foolishness" in your sight (1 Corinthians 3:19).
I pray that you will give us both "the wisdom that comes from heaven"
that is "first of all pure" (James 3:17).
Help my son to understand that
"knowledge of the Holy One is understanding" (Proverbs 9:10).
If he knows you, he has all that he needs!

Give him grace to know that "all the treasures of wisdom and knowledge" are hidden in Christ (Colossians 2:2–3) so that he turns his heart to you!

Through your Word, make him "wise for salvation through faith in Christ Jesus" (2 Timothy 3:15).

Help him to be "wise about what is good, and innocent about what is evil" (Romans 16:19).

Lord Jesus, just as you "grew in wisdom and stature, and in favor with God and man" (Luke 2:52), I ask that my son would grow in you in every way.

Let him shine so brightly with your wisdom that he will "lead many to righteousness" (Daniel 12:3).

Thank you, Father, that this is a prayer you love to answer!

Thank you that you give wisdom when we ask, because you are the source of it!

"To the only wise God be glory forever through Jesus Christ! Amen" (Romans 16:27).

———

Pray that God will bring new wisdom into your prodigal's life through His Word and His Spirit, so that he or she may long for the Lord and turn to Him.

DAY 58

Wonderful Light

But you are a chosen people, a royal priesthood, a holy nation,
God's special possession, that you may declare the praises of
him who called you out of darkness into his wonderful light.

1 PETER 2:9

I always leave the light on at night for my son, Father.
I do it to let him know he is welcome, and to show him he is loved.
I also ask for your light to fall upon his path and lead him home.
Let him see your light from the distance and be drawn to you.
Let him praise you because you "called" him
    "out of darkness into" your "wonderful light."
Even though he now sits "in darkness,"
    I ask that you will be his light (Micah 7:8).
I praise you that there is no darkness so black
    that you cannot show him the way out of it.
Bring him to the place where he can say, "You, LORD, are my lamp;
    the LORD turns my darkness into light" (2 Samuel 22:29).
Your light is wonderful, Lord.
You are "the Ancient of Days" (Daniel 7:22).
Day and night, darkness and light have been under your control
    since before time began.
You see in the dark!
Even the "darkness is as light to you" (Psalm 139:12),
    and in you "there is no darkness at all" (1 John 1:5).
You know the way for my son to come home so that he will be a son

"of the light" and a son "of the day" (1 Thessalonians 5:5)—
your son!

Then he will "walk in" your light (Isaiah 2:5) in this world and the next,
until he comes to the city that "does not need the sun or the moon to
shine on it," because your glory "gives it light" (Revelation 21:23).

Be his light and his hope, Lord Jesus! You are "the light of all mankind"
(John 1:4).

Thank you, Father, for shining your light "in the darkness" (John 1:5)
and for leaving the light on for my son.

Lead him out of "the dominion of darkness" and "into the kingdom of the
Son" you love, "in whom we have redemption, the forgiveness of sins"
(Colossians 1:13–14).

Then we will declare your praises together forever (1 Peter 2:9),
because you turned our night into everlasting day.

———

When the sun is shining, let it fall on your face. Pray your prodigal will know
the warmth and light of God's love shining within.

Back to Flame

A bruised reed he will not break,
and a smoldering wick he will not snuff out.

ISAIAH 42:3

She had more faith once, Father. Remember?

It was beautiful to see: the simple, heartfelt faith of a child.

She loved you, and the little candle of her faith burned brightly for
all to see.

But then the winds came.

Even though I tried to shield the flame of her faith from the world's
incessant blowing, my hands could only do so much.

That's why I'm placing her in your hands again today, Lord Jesus.

I can't imagine anything more fragile than "a smoldering wick."

I thank you that you "will not snuff out" this candle,
which is my daughter's faith.

Protect and nurture it, Father, so that it will glow brightly once again.

I ask for you to surround her and shield her faith from the world
(Psalm 5:12).

Rebuke the world's wind and storms the way you did long ago:
"Quiet! Be still!" (Mark 4:39).

Then she will look on you with awe, just like the disciples did.

I pray you will protect her fragile faith in every way so that she can
"stand against the devil's schemes" (Ephesians 6:11).

Father, I pray you will send someone she trusts
to tell her "the good news about Jesus" again (Acts 8:35).

I ask that her heart will be open, and that through your loving Spirit, she will
    receive the good news "with full conviction" (1 Thessalonians 1:5 RSV).
I pray that faith will permeate her life in a fresh and bold new way,
    and that she will live it out consistently.
Help her to see that "the kingdom of God is not a matter of talk
    but of power" (1 Corinthians 4:20).
I pray she "may have power, together with all the Lord's holy people, to
    grasp how wide and long and high and deep is" your love so that she
    may be "filled to the measure" of all your fullness (Ephesians 3:18–19).
Then, let her "fan into flame" every gift you've given her so that the candle
    of her faith will burn brightly once again (2 Timothy 1:6).
Let her shine so brightly that others "can see the light" (Luke 8:16)
    and come to you!
I praise you, Lord, that in your hands even a smoldering wick
    can come to life again.
I pray in your name that her faith will burn brightly!

———

Think of a time when your own faith was faltering, and God brought you
through. Praise Him that He is able do the same for your prodigal!

Dressed in Armor

*Put on the full armor of God, so that you
can take your stand against the devil's schemes.*

EPHESIANS 6:11

We need to dress my son, Lord. Just like I did when he was little,
   only this time with armor.
Your armor. Armor made especially for him.
He doesn't know how to put it on himself yet,
   so I ask your help to put it on him. He needs it more than he knows.
He's been walking too close to where the enemy walks, and he's in danger.
Show him "your ways, LORD, teach" him "your paths" (Psalm 25:4).
Help him to "stand firm" in your truth, with the "belt of truth buckled"
   around his waist (Ephesians 6:14).
I pray he will "love the truth and so be saved" (2 Thessalonians 2:10).
I see the "breastplate of righteousness" in your Word, Father
   (Ephesians 6:14).
Please put it on him.
Just as Abraham believed you, "and it was credited to him as righteousness,
   and he was called" your "friend" (James 2:23),
   I pray my son will believe *you*, Lord Jesus, and know you as
   his friend.
You said, "You are my friends if you do what I command" (John 15:14).
   I pray that he will *want* to be your friend and that he will obey you!
Then let his feet be "fitted with the readiness that comes
   from the gospel of peace" (Ephesians 6:15).

Make him ready to tell others about you.

Right now he's working on his testimony, he just doesn't know it yet!

I "take up the shield of faith," Father,

to "extinguish all the flaming arrows of the evil one" (Ephesians 6:16).

I would step in front of my son if I could,

and I *do* know that my prayers protect him.

But I also ask that he will learn to use the shield for himself.

In order to do that, he needs to "take the helmet of salvation" (Ephesians 6:17), and I pray with all of my heart that he will.

Then give him "the sword of the Spirit,

which is the word of God" (Ephesians 6:17).

May he love your Word, Lord!

Help him to use it whenever he is tempted, so he may stand his ground.

Let him "pray in the Spirit on all occasions with all kinds of prayers and requests" (Ephesians 6:18), by having his mind

"set on what the Spirit desires" (Romans 8:5).

Give him grace to understand the power of prayer and the eternal difference it makes in his life and the lives of others.

Please, use this prayer to make a difference in his life today!

The most forgotten part of the armor of God is prayer (Ephesians 6:18). Ask God to help you surround your prodigal with prayer more than ever before.

When Angels Sing

In the same way, I tell you, there is rejoicing in the presence
of the angels of God over one sinner who repents.

LUKE 15:10

I ask that he will make angels sing, Father.

I pray he will turn from his past and run with an open heart and mind
to you!

I can imagine the joy.

My joy here on earth would only be part of a much larger celebration,
because "There is rejoicing in the presence of the angels of God over
one sinner who repents" (Luke 15:10).

Your Word tells of "thousands upon thousands of angels" joyfully praising
you (Hebrews 12:22), and so they should!

"You are worthy, our Lord and God, to receive glory and honor and power,
for you created all things, and by your will they were created and have
their being" (Revelation 4:11).

You created my son and gave him life.

You long for him with an everlasting love.

You loved him so much that you gave your "one and only Son, that whoever
believes in him shall not perish but have eternal life" (John 3:16).

No wonder the angels sing when one sinner repents!

I pray that my son will know the joy of repentance, Lord.

Not just the joy of the angels or my joy, but especially *yours* and *his*!

You want "everyone to come to repentance" (2 Peter 3:9),
and you will welcome him with opens arms as he draws near.

Then, like the father in the story of the prodigal son, you "bring the best robe and put it on him" (Luke 15:22)—a robe of righteousness!

You throw a party in heaven and the angels sing!

And the joy that you have—your pure, perfect joy—shows up on his face.

He is safe and home, "set free from sin" (Romans 6:22) to serve you and love you forever, restored to the joy of a right relationship with you, free at last!

I pray he will give his heart to you soon, Lord!

Then let him make the angels continue to sing by bringing others to you.

I pray that he may be active in sharing his faith, so that he will have a full "knowledge of every good thing which is in" you (Philemon 6 NASB).

I can almost hear the music playing, Father.

Please let it begin for him today!

———

Think of the joy you've felt at times in your prodigal's life (at birth, milestones, etc.). Imagine the joy that will resound in heaven when your prodigal "comes home" to the Lord and, by faith, praise God in advance for it!

DAY 62

For the Keeping of Angels

See that you do not despise one of these little ones. For I tell you that
their angels in heaven always see the face of my Father in heaven.

MATTHEW 18:10

Your Word says you send your angels to do your "bidding,"
    Father (Psalm 103:20).
Thank you for giving our children angels who "always see" your face.
Thank you for all the times you've looked after my child when I could not:
    the near misses, the fraction-of-a-second, happened-too-fast-for-me-to-
    react moments when your angel intervened.
My child needs the protection of your angels now, Lord.
Just like when you sent one to watch over Daniel
    and "shut the mouths of the lions" (Daniel 6:22).
I need your angels to go where I cannot go, just as you did the nights
    you rescued Peter "from Herod's clutches" (Acts 12:11)
    and "opened the doors of the jail" for the apostles (Acts 5:19).
I know some might think it presumptuous of me to ask for angels for
    someone who is not where he's supposed to be, but you've done
    this before.
You did it for Elijah when he "was afraid and ran for his life" (1 Kings 19:3).
    "All at once an angel touched him," not once,
    but twice (1 Kings 19:5, 7).
You also had your angels take Lot's hand "when he hesitated" to leave
    Sodom with his family, because you were "merciful to them"
    (Genesis 19:16).

You are merciful, Lord! And you said that "whatever you loose on earth
will be loosed in heaven" (Matthew 18:18).

So I ask that you send an angel from heaven to help my son.

Just as "some who have done this have entertained angels without
realizing it" (Hebrews 13:2 NLT), let a stranger show him
a kindness that he knows is from you.

Or, as when you sent your angels to shepherds with the "good news" of
Jesus (Luke 2:10), send someone to share your love and your presence
with him so that he will believe, seek you out, and bow before you.

You've said that "the angel of the LORD encamps around those who fear
him, and he delivers them" (Psalm 34:7).

Because I "know what it is to fear" you (2 Corinthians 5:11), Lord,
with reverence, awe, and love, I ask that you deliver my son.

Your Word tells me about what you've done for those you call your own:
"In all their distress he too was distressed, and the angel of his presence
saved them. In his love and mercy he redeemed them" (Isaiah 63:9).

Redeem my son, Lord! Let him be a joy to you and to all of heaven,
because "there is rejoicing in the presence of the angels of God
over one sinner who repents" (Luke 15:10).

I don't know how you will do it, but I ask you to help him open his heart
to you.

I'd love to know how you're going to do it, Lord, but I know that
"even angels long to look into these things" (1 Peter 1:12).

So I will watch and pray and wait, and say with the angels,
"Praise and glory and wisdom and thanks and honor and power and
strength be to our God for ever and ever. Amen!" (Revelation 7:11–12).

**Was there a time in your life where God kept you safe in danger? Remember
it before Him, and thank Him that He is able to do the same for your prodigal.**

Quiet in His Love

The LORD your God is with you, the Mighty Warrior who saves.
He will take great delight in you; in his love he will
no longer rebuke you, but will rejoice over you with singing.

ZEPHANIAH 3:17

"The LORD your God is with you, the Mighty Warrior who saves. He will
take great delight in you; in his love he will no longer rebuke you, but
will rejoice over you with singing."

What beautiful thoughts, Lord.

You are all of those things!

You *are* "with [me]."

You *are* "the Mighty Warrior who saves."

The thought of you taking delight in me and comforting me with your love
gives my soul hope that this world cannot take away.

When I imagine you rejoicing over me with singing, I'm reminded that you
are my Father, and I am your child (1 John 5:19).

"See what great love the Father has lavished on us, that we should be called
children of God! And that is what we are!" (1 John 3:1).

When my daughter was little, Father, I *rejoiced* over her with singing.

There were lullabies and happy songs, and quiet moments just between us.

How good it was just to hold her in my arms
and feel the softness of her cheek next to mine.

What a gift she was, Father, and still is!

Even though she has made choices that have grieved me and grieved you, I
cannot give up on her.

I will "keep on praying" (Ephesians 6:18) until she is restored to a right
 relationship with you.
Then when she comes home to you, I will pray some more,
 praising you for what you have done!
In the "quietness and confidence" that comes from you alone (Isaiah 32:17), I
 will wait and watch and pray.
You are "the God who gives endurance and encouragement" (Romans 15:5).
Your love will go the distance to bring her home.
Let it happen soon, Lord!
I can hardly wait to see her face reflecting your love and goodness and
 grace, because you make your "face shine on" her (Numbers 6:25).
Because of your kindness and mercy I "do not lose heart" (2 Corinthians 4:1).
I'm lifted by the vision of *you* being with her, taking "great delight" in her,
 quieting her with your love, and rejoicing over her "with singing."
You *are* mighty to save, Father!
All of my hope is in you.

———

**Sit quietly before the Lord and simply tell Him you love Him. Ask the Lord
to help your prodigal be able to grasp "how wide and long and high and
deep is the love of Christ" (see Ephesians 3:16–19).**

Who Sinned?

His disciples asked him, "Rabbi, who sinned,
this man or his parents, that he was born blind?"

JOHN 9:2

One Saturday afternoon, when my sister came home from college, she went out to lunch at a local restaurant with Dad. They were holding hands across the table and talking intently when the phone rang at home.

My mother answered the phone. It was a lady from our church.

"Mrs. Banks, do you know where your husband is right now? It is my Christian duty to inform you that he is having lunch with some blond *thing*."

Mom, who knew exactly where Dad was, decided to play along: "Is he doing that again?"

"You mean he's done it before?"

"Oh, yes. Thank you for telling me. Good-bye."

That was the end of the conversation.

The next morning, Mom had the family wait on the church's front steps after worship. When the woman who had called her came out the front doors, Mom pointed to my sister and said with a smile, "I'd like to introduce you to my daughter."

Have you ever jumped to conclusions without knowing all of the facts? That's what the disciples were doing when they encountered a blind man and asked Jesus, "Rabbi, who sinned, this man or his parents, that he was born blind?"

God promises in His Word that "the child will not share the guilt of the parent, nor will the parent share the guilt of the child" (Ezekiel 18:20). But as the disciples' question demonstrated, many in Jesus's day believed that sickness was the direct result of sin either in the life of the one who was ill or his parents.

Jesus's response to the disciples speaks volumes: "Neither this man nor his parents sinned . . . but this happened so that the works of God might be displayed in his life" (John 9:3). While the disciples were busy looking for sin and someone to blame, Jesus saw an opportunity to show the greatness and the love of God. Sometimes the parents of prodigals may find themselves thinking like the disciples. We look for someone to blame, and we don't look very far. More than one parent of a prodigal son or daughter has found themselves asking, "Is God punishing me through my child for something I did in the past?" Fortunately, Jesus's response to the disciples and God's promise through Ezekiel indicate that the answer to that question is an emphatic "No."

God's promise through Ezekiel makes it clear that each of us must take responsibility for our own actions. We cannot blame parents or genetics for our sins. We also cannot blame ourselves for the sinful choices of a son or daughter. Still, that's not always easy.

There have been times when I've heard my parents' words coming out of my mouth when I talk to my children (the words *"Because I said so!"* come to mind). I've also heard the words I spoke to my parents coming out of my children's mouths. When those words are hurtful, I've caught myself thinking, "This sounds *too* familiar. Is my past coming back to haunt me? Is God judging me for my own rebellion by giving me a rebellious child? Is this my *payback?*"

Thankfully, God doesn't see it that way. His promise is worth repeating and taking to heart: "The son [will] not share the guilt of his father" (see Ezekiel 18:20). I take great comfort in that, because I don't want my children to bear the burden of things I did long ago. It's also good to know that God isn't holding them against me.

The spiritual blindness in our children's lives is not caused by sins of the parents but by sin that is part of the fallen nature we all share, because "all have sinned and fall short of the glory of God" (Romans 3:23). That sin has consequences, and we must repent of it and leave it at the foot of the cross. But before that can happen for our prodigal children, Jesus must open their eyes.

It's encouraging that Jesus came of his own initiative to the man who was blind from birth. The man didn't ask for Jesus's help. Jesus sought *him* out. He *stopped* and looked the man in his sightless eyes.

Jesus is also able to encounter our children when they are not looking for Him. God has ways of reaching our children that we've never thought of. Jesus loves our prodigal kids and wants to display the work of God in their lives, no matter what they've done. "God demonstrates his own love for us in this: While we were still sinners, Christ died for us" (Romans 5:8). Jesus wants to touch our children and set them free, so they will become witnesses to the Father's kindness and power, and one day love others into the kingdom.

Our prodigals don't know it yet, but right now they're just working on their testimonies.

Jesus is coming their way, and someday they will tell of all he has done for them, just like another young man long ago. One day, "the eyes" of their hearts will "be enlightened" (Ephesians 1:18), and his words will be theirs: "One thing I do know. I was blind but now I see!" (John 9:25).

> *There is no place where earth's sorrows*
> *are more felt than up in heaven;*
> *there is no place where earth's failings*
> *have such kindly judgment given.*

—FREDERICK W. FABER,
"THERE'S A WIDENESS IN GOD'S MERCY"

DAY 64

Sins of the Parents?

As he went along, he saw a man blind from birth. His disciples asked him,
"Rabbi, who sinned, this man or his parents, that he was born blind?"

JOHN 9:1-2

Sometimes I feel like asking the same question that was on the mind of
  the disciples, Lord: "Who sinned? This man or his parents?"
At times I've wondered if the spiritual blindness in my son's life
  is because of some sin I committed in the past.
Thank you, Father, that you don't see it that way at all.
There was a time when you would punish "the children for the sin of
  the parents to the third and fourth generation" (Numbers 14:18),
  but no longer.
You've done something entirely new!
You promise in your Word that "the child will not share the guilt
  of the parent, nor will the parent share the guilt of the child."
You say that you will judge "each [one] according to [his] ways."
Thank you, Father, that through your mercy we can have
  "a new heart and a new spirit" (Ezekiel 18:20, 30–31).
I understand that we are all "born blind," because through Adam's sin,
  "sin entered the world" (Romans 5:12),
  and "all have sinned and fall short" of your glory (Romans 3:23).
"There is no one righteous, not even one" (Romans 3:10).
But you promise, "I will give you a new heart and put a new spirit in you."
You even say, "I will put *my Spirit* in you
  and move you to follow my decrees" (Ezekiel 36:26–27).

I praise you that you opened for us "a new and living way" (Hebrews
	10:20) through your Son!
You have "given us the Spirit as a deposit,
	guaranteeing what is to come" (2 Corinthians 5:5).
Thank you that your Word assures us, "The promise is for you and your
	children and for all who are far off—for all whom the Lord our God
	will call" (Acts 2:39).
My child is far off, Lord, just like I was. Please call him.
Let him hear your voice beckoning him to come home.
I praise you that you "do not hold against us
	the sins of past generations" (Psalm 79:8).
"With you there is forgiveness" (Psalm 130:4).
Though we are born spiritually blind, in your mercy you touch us and
	open our eyes so that we can "see wonderful things" (Psalm 119:18).
Just as you did for that young man who was born "blind from birth,"
	I ask that you look on my son with your love and compassion.
Oh Lord, please let my son see the wonder of all that you are today!

———

**Ask God to lift any thoughts of "if only I had done something different with
my prodigal" from your heart. Praise Him that new beginnings are always
possible with Him, for your prodigal and for you!**

Strength to Go On

Though the fig tree does not bud and there are no grapes on the vines,
though the olive crop fails and the fields produce no food,
though there are no sheep in the pen and no cattle in the stalls,
yet I will rejoice in the LORD, I will be joyful in God my Savior.

HABAKKUK 3:17–19

I will remind myself of this, Lord:
>It's always good to praise you, regardless of how I feel at the moment.

"For great is the LORD and most worthy of praise" (1 Chronicles 16:25).

"I *will* rejoice in the LORD. I *will* be joyful in God" (Habakkuk 3:18),
>regardless of my external circumstances on any given day.
>And *why not?*

Yes, times are difficult with my child. She's running from me
>and from you.

My heart aches. I long to take her in my arms and protect her from harm, if
>only she would have it.

Then I am reminded of your Word and your promise:
>"Yet the LORD longs to be gracious to you;
>therefore he will rise up to show you compassion" (Isaiah 30:18).

There's a lot of meaning in that one word, *yet*. You know how I feel,
>don't you?

Not only about my daughter. About the whole human race.

That's why you came, why you sent *your* one and only son:
>"We all, like sheep, have gone astray, each of us has turned to our own
>way; and the LORD has laid on him the iniquity of us all" (Isaiah 53:6).

Not only do you understand but you've also faced our rebellion with a heart
that feels with more "depth" than I could ever know (Romans 11:33).
I praise you for that and will wait for you, because "since ancient times no
one has heard, no ear has perceived, no eye has seen any God besides
you, who acts on behalf of those who wait for him" (Isaiah 64:4).
Even though my daughter is far away from you right now,
"surely the arm of the LORD is not too short to save" (Isaiah 59:1).
You *want* to draw her close. You have told us in your Word that
"the promise is for you and your children and for all who are far off—
for all whom the Lord our God will call" (Acts 2:39).
I hold on to that promise, and I hold on to you.
I choose to praise you and hope in you because it's the best course of action
and you deserve it. And you bless us all the more when we trust in you.
"Those who hope in the LORD will renew their strength" (Isaiah 40:31).
"Blessed are those who have learned to acclaim you" (Psalm 89:15).
"Blessed are those whose strength is in you" (Psalm 84:5).
I am blessed, Lord. You are my blessing!
And I praise you for *you*, with all my heart!

———

**Praise the Lord for His amazing power, and for His promise that those
who "wait for the Lord" (Isaiah 40:31 ESV) will be renewed with the strength
He gives.**

How Long, O Lord?

How long, LORD, how long?

PSALM 6:3

I've heard it said that I shouldn't pray for patience, Lord,
    and that if I ask for patience I'm only asking for difficulty.
I don't want to believe that it always works that way.
Better put, I don't want to believe that you always work that way.
Your Word tells me that "the LORD is good to those whose hope is
    in him, to the one who seeks him" (Lamentations 3:25).
I do hope in you, and I am seeking you this morning once again.
I know that you are faithful and that you answer prayer.
But right now I'd like to ask you (just like David did),
    "How long, LORD?"
Your Word promises, "Ask and it will be given to you; seek,
    and you will find; knock and the door will be opened to you"
    (Matthew 7:7).
Still, sometimes I feel like I've been asking and seeking and knocking
    at that door for days on end, and it still stays shut and locked.
Now is one of those times. I feel stuck between how-it-is and how-it-
    could-be.
I'd love to see a change in my child's heart and life, and I do trust that
    you will make that happen, but it hasn't happened yet.
I don't want to sound like I'm "complaining," Father (Philippians 2:14 NLT),
    or to be like those who grumbled against you in the wilderness
    (Numbers 14:29).

You know my heart completely as I come to you in prayer (2 Chronicles 6:30).

You know that what I'm doing is *longing*.

"I long for your salvation, LORD" (Psalm 119:174).

I long to see my son's heart filled with the joy you alone can give (Psalm 4:7).

I long to see him "turn from evil and do good" (Psalm 34:14).

Like the father who saw his prodigal coming home "while he was still a long way off" (Luke 15:20), I'm watching and waiting.

I'm "looking for your salvation" (Psalm 119:123).

My "eyes look to the LORD our God, till he shows us his mercy" (Psalm 123:2).

Lord Jesus, just like others who called out to you before and kept calling until an answer came, I'm crying out to you: "Lord, Son of David, have mercy on us!" (Matthew 20:30–31).

I'm placing all of my hope in you and asking for the patience to keep hoping, keep watching, keep calling . . . no matter how long it takes.

I praise you in advance for the day your purpose will be fulfilled in my son's life.

I praise you for the day he and I will say together, "Today salvation has come to this house. . . . For the Son of Man came to seek and to save the lost" (Luke 19:9–10).

———

"How long, Lord?" is a prayer that occurs several places in Scripture. Thank God that His Word shows us that we can pray that way, and ask Him to bring your prodigal "home" to Him soon.

When You're "Prayed Out"

Who then is the one who condemns? No one. Christ Jesus,
who died—more than that, who was raised to life—is at
the right hand of God and is also interceding for us.

ROMANS 8:34

Sometimes I feel too numb to pray, Father.
It's not that I don't believe you answer prayer. I do believe.
But sometimes when I pray and pray and don't see any change
    in my child, I lose heart.
Please forgive my impatience and lack of faith, Lord.
Help me to take your Word to heart, that we "should always pray
    and not give up" (Luke 18:1).
When the woman kept knocking on the door of the "unjust judge"
    (Luke 18:6), she got what she asked for.
When the Canaanite woman pleaded with you for her daughter,
    and the disciples tried to send her away,
      you *did* grant the woman's request (Matthew 15:25–28).
When the man knocked on his friend's door after midnight,
    and the friend wanted him to go away,
      you said "because of his friend's shameless boldness, he will get up
      and give him as much as he needs" (Luke 11:8 CSB).
Help me to be bold, Lord! Especially now!
My daughter needs me to be, and I know you want me to be.
I want to thank you that you help me to pray.
    I especially need that help right now.

Thank you that you are "at the right hand" of the Father,
    "interceding for us" (Romans 8:34).
Holy Spirit, I praise you that you are praying for me and my child
    "with groanings too deep for words" (Romans 8:26 ESV).
Lord Jesus, I thank you that when my faith is lacking,
    you "will remain faithful" (2 Timothy 2:13).
I praise you that "faith as small as a mustard seed" can move mountains
    (Matthew 17:20). I have that!
My faith may be small right now, but it's enough when I place it in
    your hands.
So I place my daughter in your hands again, no matter how challenging
    things may be.
You said it yourself: "With people it is impossible, but not with God"
    (Luke 18:27), and "all things are possible with God" (Mark 10:27 NASB).
I hold on to those promises right now, and praise you that "no matter how
    many promises God has made, they are 'Yes' in Christ" (2 Corinthians
    1:20).
I will keep coming to you, Lord, and keep praying. How can I not?
Your "Yes!" is all I need.

———————

**Thank the Lord that even when you don't know what to say when you pray,
He understands the desires of your heart.**

When He Is Older

Start children off on the way they should go,
and when they are old they will not turn from it.

PROVERBS 22:6

I can see him years from now, Father. When my prayers have been
answered, and his heart has turned to you.

I can see him standing strong, "a good man, full of the Holy Spirit and
faith" (Acts 11:24).

For that to happen, I know I need to do my best to
build a "firm foundation" (1 Timothy 6:19) for him, Father.

Of all of the things I may do for my child, I understand that nothing is
more important than sharing your love with him, not just "with words
or speech but with actions and in truth" (1 John 3:18).

Even though this is a challenging time in his life, help me to
"be prepared in season and out of season" so that I may
"correct, rebuke and encourage—with great patience
and careful instruction" (2 Timothy 4:2).

I praise you for the truth that if I raise him "in the way he should go,"
"when he is old he will not depart from it" (Proverbs 22:6 ESV).

I want to help him "take hold of the life that is truly life" (1 Timothy 6:19).

Let him be spared the pain and difficulty of years lived apart from you, and
give his heart to you soon!

You tell us we "must be ready," because you "will come at an hour when" we
"do not expect" (Matthew 24:44).

I pray he *will* be ready and will give his heart to you today!

You promise that your Word will not return to you empty, "but will accomplish what" you "desire and achieve the purpose for which" you "sent it" (Isaiah 55:11).

I pray that you will help me as I communicate your Word and your love to my son.

Help me to make the good news of Jesus as clear to him as I possibly can.

Give him "ears to hear" your Word as I share it with him so that he truly listens (Mark 4:9).

Let him not only "listen to the word," but help him to "do what it says" and follow you in obedience and love (James 1:22).

I love my son, Lord, and I thank you for entrusting him to me.

I know you have given him to me so that I may point him to you.

You are "the God who gives life to the dead and calls into being things that were not" (Romans 4:17).

I pray you will raise him to life in you and call him your own!

I can see the day coming by faith when he's "filled to the measure of all the fullness" you want to give him (Ephesians 3:19).

And I praise you because you are "faithful," and you "will do it" (1 Thessalonians 5:24).

Imagine your prodigal being older and wiser in the Lord, and ask the Lord to make this possible (see Matthew 19:26).

When Sorrow and Sighing Flee Away

And those the LORD rescued will return.
They will enter Zion with singing;
everlasting joy will crown their heads.
Gladness and joy will overtake them,
and sorrow and sighing will flee away.

ISAIAH 35:10

What a day that will be, Lord!
The day my daughter comes home to you,
    rescued, forgiven, restored, and blessed.
I can almost hear her singing!
I long for your "everlasting joy" to crown her
    and for her to find soul satisfaction in you!
I can imagine what the day will be like, Lord.
I can see your "gladness and joy" keeping pace behind her,
    getting closer and closer until they completely overtake her
    and she finds the desire of her heart in you.
I can also see "sorrow and sighing" flee away as each of the world's
    hurts and deceptions are scattered "in the light of your presence"
    (Psalm 90:8), and the truth and beauty of all that you are
    "shines forth" (Psalm 50:2).
I praise you, Father, for what you will do.

I pray that even now you will prepare my daughter's heart for it: remove every resistance, overcome every argument, expose every allure and false affection until she comes to understand that you are her deepest need and greatest hope.

Let nothing hold her back, Lord!

You said, "whatever you loose on earth will be loosed in heaven" (Matthew 16:19).

Release her from every constraint that keeps her from coming to you.

Let loose every blessing you have waiting that will draw her heart to you.

You say in your perfect wisdom, "I love those who love me, and those who seek me find me" (Proverbs 8:17).

Let her seek you, find you, and love you, Lord!

I praise you, Lord Jesus, that you came to give your life as a ransom for many (Mark 10:45).

I pray with all my heart that my daughter will be among the rescued who sing for joy as they return to you!

———————

Pray your prodigal will come to realize that choices he or she has made are not worth the pain they have caused, and turn to Jesus for the peace only He can give.

More Than I Ask or Imagine

*Now to him who is able to do immeasurably more than
all we ask or imagine, according to his power that is at work
within us, to him be glory in the church and in Christ Jesus
throughout all generations, for ever and ever! Amen.*

EPHESIANS 3:20–21

I can imagine the difference you will make in my son's life
    on the day he comes back to you.
But I praise you that no matter what I'm looking forward to,
    you are "able to do *immeasurably more* than all" I "ask or imagine."
Thank you, almighty Father, for "things too wonderful for me
    to know" (Job 42:3).
My prayer is that my son will be among the "generations" who praise you
    "for ever and ever," but you can even do more than that! You can even
    use him to lead others to you!
Your "plan is wonderful" and your "wisdom is magnificent" (Isaiah 28:29).
"I am your servant" (1 Kings 18:36), Lord. I want to serve you in any way
    you want in order to help my son draw closer to you.
I ask that you "give me discernment" for whatever you desire (Psalm
    119:125).
I pray that you will convict him of any sin in his life
    that holds him back from coming to you.
I pray that he will be "cleansed from" his "past sins" (2 Peter 1:9) by
    confessing them to you and finding mercy through "the blood of Jesus"
    that "purifies us from all sin" (1 John 1:7).

Let him understand deeply in his heart that you sent Jesus to save him,
    because "if anyone acknowledges that Jesus is the Son of God," you
    will live "in them and they in" you (1 John 4:15).
Father, because you gave your son to me and held nothing back,
    I give my son to you.
It is only right, because he was your gift to me to begin with.
    "Every life belongs to" you (Ezekiel 18:4 CSB).
Revive my son, Lord! Breathe the breath of eternal life into his soul.
"This is eternal life: that" he may "know you, the only true God,
    and Jesus Christ, whom you have sent" (John 17:3).
"Many, LORD my God, are the wonders you have done" (Psalm 40:5).
Do another, Father! I pray not only that my son will come to life in you
    today, but that you would not stop there!
Do "immeasurably more" because "nothing is too hard for you"
    (Jeremiah 32:17).

———

Praise the Lord for His infinite creativity and that His ability to bring our prodigals home to Him is not limited by our imaginations!

The Good Shepherd

The Pharisees and the teachers of the law muttered, "This man welcomes sinners and eats with them." Then Jesus told them this parable: "Suppose one of you has a hundred sheep and loses one of them. Doesn't he leave the ninety-nine in the open country and go after the lost sheep until he finds it? And when he finds it, he joyfully puts it on his shoulders and goes home. Then he calls his friends and neighbors together and says, 'Rejoice with me; I have found my lost sheep.' I tell you that in the same way there will be more rejoicing in heaven over one sinner who repents than over ninety-nine righteous persons who do not need to repent."

LUKE 15:2–7

It's a long road between Amarillo and Albuquerque. Especially when your kids are at that "are we there yet?" age.

But this was a quiet moment. Geoffrey was asleep (finally!), Cari was driving, and Katie and I were in the backseat, watching the lines go by on the pavement.

Katie doesn't sleep much in the car. She gets that from me. Cari and Geoff can zonk out anywhere. Katie and I are wired differently.

It was the middle of the morning. We had started early to beat the desert heat. Cari tried to be helpful: "Why don't you two just close your eyes and go to sleep?"

She could just as easily have told us to strap ourselves to the roof rack— we were as wide-eyed as if we had done just that. We had gone through all of Katie's books, played with her Barbies, and sung every song we could remember. But I-40 was merciless. It just kept going in one . . . straight . . . very long . . . line.

Then Katie came up with a new idea.

"Daddy, will you tell me a story?"

Katie loved my stories, and she knew I loved telling them to her. Suddenly the ride became interesting for both of us. The stories came in rapid succession.

"Tell me another!"

On and on it went, until Dad's creative well began to run dry. "I can't think of anything else right now, Katie."

"Are you sure? C'mon, Dad! Just one more! Don't you know any other stories?"

"Well, there is one. And it isn't just any story. It's the best story of all, because it's true."

I had shared the good news about Jesus with Katie several times before, but this time was different. I sensed that she was grasping the words and taking them to heart, and God was enabling me to explain the gospel with a clarity that could have come only from Him. His Spirit was at work. I could feel it.

I explained the story of salvation to her from creation to Easter, and she listened intently. When I asked her if she believed it was true, she nodded her head. When I asked, "Would you like to ask Jesus to come into your heart and take your sins away?" her response was an immediate "Yes!"

We bowed our heads and she began to pray with words that were simple but sincere. It was a precious moment that I will remember as long as I live. Cari and I understood in that moment that God was doing something very special in our daughter's life, even in her tender years.

Sometimes that moment seems like a lifetime ago, even though it was only a little over a decade. Katie is in college now, and the choices she made during adolescence were sometimes heartbreaking. Some nights we were reminded of what a friend—a church planter like myself (i.e., a pastor who starts a new church)—had told us: "Being a church planter is like painting a target on your back and saying to the devil, 'Come get me.'" In our instance, the devil went after both of our children.

But he's not the only one who is going after them. Not only are Cari and I pursuing them with our prayers, we're doing our best to keep up with the Good Shepherd as he takes strides to bring them back to the fold.

Jesus's parable of the lost sheep in Luke 15:1–7 is just as much about the shepherd as it is about the sheep. He feels such a sense of loss when he discovers that he's missing a sheep that he leaves ninety-nine sheep in "open country" to go after one. "And when he finds it, he joyfully puts it on his shoulders and goes home." Then he calls his friends and throws a party. Jesus wraps up the parable by saying, "I tell you that in the same way there will be more rejoicing in heaven over one sinner who repents than over ninety-nine righteous persons who do not need to repent."

That kind of joy tells me something. The Good Shepherd won't give up looking, even if it takes a lifetime. Though the way is long and hard and uphill, He'll persevere. He knows where His sheep are, and He will find the way to them.

So we must do our best to stay close to Him while the search continues. When He will bring them home, we do not know. We just know that He's looking. And that should give us the hope we need to go on.

Even though His sheep has strayed, he or she could be close, just over the next hill. The Good Shepherd knows, and He has a way of surprising us.

I've seen His work before.

Heading west on I-40, I saw the badlands open out into Promised Land. The answer to our prayers could be just around the bend.

Do not be afraid, for I am with you;
I will bring your children from the east and gather you
from the west. I will say to the north, "Give them up!"
and to the south, "Do not hold them back."

—ISAIAH 43:5–6

Your Dream for My Child

And afterward, I will pour out my Spirit on all people.
Your sons and daughters will prophesy,
your old men will dream dreams,
your young men will see visions.

JOEL 2:28

Father, you have a vision for my child that is beautiful beyond words.

Your "plan is wonderful," and your "wisdom is magnificent" (Isaiah 28:29).

I can only imagine what you have planned for her!

I have so many dreams for my child, Father.

I believe I want good things for her. But my wisdom is limited,
   and my heart has been tainted by sin.

So I want what you want, Lord. Your vision for her, your dream
   for her future!

There is no sin in you (1 John 3:5). Your way is perfect (2 Samuel 22:31).

You have promised, "Call to me and I will answer you and tell you great
   and unsearchable things you do not know" (Jeremiah 33:3).

I do call to you for her, and thank you that you will answer.

It's not so much that I need to know your vision for her life
   as *she needs to know it.*

She needs to "taste and see" that you are good (Psalm 34:8).

She needs to know that you are "a refuge in times of trouble,"
   and that you care for "those who trust" in you (Nahum 1:7).

She has an adversary that you know so much better than I, even though
   "we are not unaware of his schemes" (2 Corinthians 2:11).

Father, I ask in the strong name of Jesus that you frustrate every plan
that the enemy has against my daughter.

I long to see your Spirit bless my child, Father, while she is still young.

Let her be happy in you, and let her heart give her joy and the wisdom to
know that she will one day stand before you.

She needs to acknowledge you in all her ways so that you will make
her "paths straight" (Proverbs 3:6) and keep her "from the snares"
(Proverbs 14:27) that would bring her harm.

Lord Jesus, I pray that she will learn from you, for you are "gentle and
humble in heart."

In you, she will "find rest" for her soul (Matthew 11:29).

Be her rest, Lord, and her "peace" (Ephesians 2:14).

Be her life and her purpose, her ultimate goal. This is your dream for
my child.

"Blessed" is she "whose help is the God of Jacob,
whose hope is in the LORD" (Psalm 146:5).

Oh, Lord, be her help and her hope!

Father, please give my daughter grace and insight to turn to you!

———

What dreams does God have for your prodigal?

Ask Him to help you want what He wants, and pray that He will help you
to be His servant in bringing them about.

Turning Hearts

He will turn the hearts of the parents to their children,
and the hearts of the children to their parents.

MALACHI 4:6

Thank you, Lord, for turning my heart to my son.
What a blessing it is to pray for him! I'm grateful for both the privilege
and the opportunity to see you move in his life in answer to prayer.
As I pray, I'm reminded of how much you love him, and of the truth that
"there is a future hope" for him that "will not be cut off" (Proverbs
24:14) because of your kindness.
Father, I'd like to ask you to turn his heart as well.
"Let [him] turn to the LORD, and he will have mercy on [him],
and to our God, for he will freely pardon" (Isaiah 55:7).
Father, the thought of being separated from my son for all eternity
is more than I can bear.
He must come to you, Father! You are "God who saves" (Psalm 68:20).
Please save him! Fill him "with all joy and peace" as he trusts in you
(Romans 15:13). Let it happen today!
I pray that you will strengthen him with power through your Spirit
in his inner being "so that Christ may dwell" in his heart through faith
(Ephesians 3:17).
Father, as you move in his heart in a special way,
I'd also like to ask that you turn his heart to me.
The past years have been difficult and have sometimes caused distance
between us.

Father, you can find the way to get through to his heart
and to let him know how much I love him.
I choose to forgive him for what has happened in the past, Lord,
just as you have forgiven me (Colossians 3:13).
Please help him also to "get rid of all bitterness" (Ephesians 4:31) toward
me, so that nothing will mar the love that we have for each other, or
for you.
Lord Jesus, long ago you prayed that all who believe in you "may be one"
(John 17:11).
I pray that one day my son and I will have "the same love,
being one in spirit and of one mind" and purpose (Philippians 2:2).
I pray that he will be "convinced that neither death nor life, neither angels
nor demons, neither the present nor the future, nor any powers,
neither height nor depth, nor anything else in all creation, will be able
to separate us from the love of God that is in Christ Jesus our Lord"
(Romans 8:38–39).
"We are more than conquerors through him who loved us" (Romans 8:37).
Your love conquers all, Lord. Conquer our hearts for you!

———

The Lord knows the way into our prodigals' hearts unlike any other.
Praise Him for this! When our words and efforts to reach our prodigals
falter, He is still able!

The Contender

But this is what the LORD says:
"Yes, captives will be taken from warriors,
and plunder retrieved from the fierce;
I will contend with those who contend with you,
and your children I will save."

ISAIAH 49:25

We've been contended with, Lord.

The enemy has assaulted my family fiercely and taken my child
"captive to do his will" (2 Timothy 2:26).

He has sent his fierce warriors to plunder my home and my hopes for my
child, but he will not succeed.

He has tried to steal that which belongs to *you.*

You made him, and I've given him to you.

Go after the enemy, Lord! "Contend with those who contend with" us!

Take back what is rightfully yours!

You told your people once, "Your children I will save."

Save my son, Father!

I pray that he will come to his "senses and escape from the trap of the devil"
(2 Timothy 2:26).

Wake him up in the enemy's camp
and "provide a way out" (1 Corinthians 10:13).

Unlock the chains on his hands and his feet and his heart, and let him run
to you!

Your Word tells me that you will pursue your "foes into the realm of darkness.

Whatever they plot against the LORD,"

you "will bring to an end" (Nahum 1:8–9).

I'm counting on that, Father. I'm counting on you!

I ask you to bring back my son and all that has been stolen from us.

Strike down the enemy and bring this matter to a firm and final end.

I can see my son returning to you, held up by your strong arms,

a captive "set free from sin" (Romans 6:18).

May he be among those who "listen to your voice" and "follow [you]."

Because you are able to "give them eternal life,"

and "no one will snatch them out of" your hand (John 10:27–28).

I pray my son will be brought into the safety of your love, Lord Jesus.

"The wicked bend their bows; they set their arrows against the strings

to shoot from the shadows" (Psalm 11:2).

But I "take up the shield of faith, with which you can extinguish

all the flaming arrows of the evil one" (Ephesians 6:16).

"Thanks be to" you, Father!

You give us "the victory through our Lord Jesus Christ" (1 Corinthians 15:57).

Let that victory come in my son's life today!

———

David called the Lord "my strong deliverer" (Psalm 140:7). Praise Him that He is able to deliver you and your prodigal from every evil, and pray that He will.

Running to Jesus

The name of the LORD is a fortified tower;
the righteous run to it and are safe.

PROVERBS 18:10

"How sweet the Name of Jesus sounds in a believer's ear!
    It soothes his sorrows, heals his wounds, and drives away
    his fear."[10]

Yes! Your name is sweet to me, Lord!

"Salvation is found in no one else, for there is no other name under heaven
    given to mankind by which we must be saved" (Acts 4:12).

I pray your name over my child today, Jesus.

There is power in your name! I call upon all that you are to bless my son
    and draw him to you.

I pray that you will be his Wonderful Counselor (Isaiah 9:6)
    who speaks to him of his need for you.

I pray you will be his "good shepherd," that he will know you and listen to
    your voice (John 10:11, 14, 16).

I pray your "goodness and love will follow" him all the days of his life,
    and he will dwell in your house forever (Psalm 23:6).

I ask you to be with him wherever he goes, because you are
    "Immanuel . . . 'God with us'" (Matthew 1:23).

You are "the Lamb of God, who takes away the sin of the world" (John
    1:29), and I plead your mercy for him.

---

10. Newton, "How Sweet the Name of Jesus Sounds," *Olney Hymns*, 58.

You are "the sacrifice that atones for our sins,"
the "advocate who pleads our case before the Father" (1 John 2:1–2 NLT).
You are "The LORD Our Righteous Savior" (Jeremiah 23:6).
I pray you will one day be all of these things to my son, and more!
I pray that he will come to you and believe, so that you will be the
"bread of life" to him, and he will "never go hungry"
and "never be thirsty" (John 6:35).
You are "the author of life" (Acts 3:15). I ask for a new start in life for
him, in which you will be "the Alpha and the Omega, the First and
the Last, the Beginning and the End" (Revelation 22:13).
Be the "bright Morning Star" (Revelation 22:16)
that rises in his heart (2 Peter 1:19).
I ask that you will be "the hope of glory" to him (Colossians 1:27),
living in him and showing him all of the good things of God.
I pray he will be "made strong" by faith in your name, Lord Jesus
(Acts 3:16).
God has given you "the name that is above every name," that at your
name "every knee should bow, in heaven and on earth and under
the earth, and every tongue acknowledge" that you are Lord
(Philippians 2:9–11).
Let him run to you, Lord, and bow his knees and his heart.
I ask that he will confess that you are Lord, call on your name,
and "be saved" (Acts 2:21).

———————

**Kneel before the Lord and praise Him, praying your favorite names for Him
in Scripture (including any from the prayer above!).**

DAY 75

Inner Beauty

Your beauty should not come from outward adornment, such as
elaborate hairstyles and the wearing of gold jewelry or fine clothes.
Rather, it should be that of your inner self, the unfading beauty of
a gentle and quiet spirit, which is of great worth in God's sight.

1 PETER 3:3–4

Everywhere she turns she feels the pressure to be beautiful, Father.
The magazines and airwaves call out to her with pitches and promises,
    but the beauty they sell is only skin-deep.
The runways show off styles that sparkle for a season
    and then end up in a thrift store.
Because even Solomon with all of his wisdom was led "astray"
    by pretty faces (1 Kings 11:3), she needs your wisdom, Lord.
Help her to see through the thin layer of skin to the heart of the matter:
    "Charm is deceptive, and beauty is fleeting;
    but a woman who fears the LORD is to be praised" (Proverbs 31:30).
Father, I pray you will turn her eyes from the world and direct them to you.
Then she "will look and be radiant," and her "heart will throb and swell
    with joy" (Isaiah 60:5), because there is no happiness like the joy
    you give!
I ask that you will give her that which matters much to you:
    "the unfading beauty of a gentle and quiet spirit."
Help her to value *inward* adornment over "outward adornment."
Let her be "clothed with strength and dignity" (Proverbs 31:25).
May her soul be "calmed and quieted" as she rests in you (Psalm 131:2).

May your light and love shine from behind her eyes, Lord Jesus,
    because you dwell in her heart "through faith" (Ephesians 3:17).
May her inner beauty be so evident
    that it becomes the first thing others notice about her.
May it be your blessing to draw them to yourself through her!
Father, I pray you will protect her from the "meaningless" (Ecclesiastes
    11:10) vanity of this world, which places an inordinate value on
    youthful beauty.
Let her know that she is valued by you
    and that your opinion matters more than any other.
That way, she will know she is always loved.
Let her "say with confidence, 'The Lord is my helper'" (Hebrews 13:6).
Let her be filled with "a glorious, inexpressible joy" because
    "the reward for trusting" you will be,
    "the salvation" of her soul (1 Peter 1:8–9 NLT).
I pray she will place her hope in you, so that the wonder of all that you
    are will make her beautiful in every way (1 Peter 3:5),
    a shining beauty, from the inside out.

———

Pray that when your prodigal looks in the mirror, that she or he will see someone who is loved by God, and turn to Him.

Every Blessing

Every good and perfect gift is from above, coming down from the Father
of the heavenly lights, who does not change like shifting shadows.

JAMES 1:17

How blessed I am, Father!
You've given me "every spiritual blessing in Christ" (Ephesians 1:3).
Every blessing! Teach me how to count those blessings, Lord,
    and to take so much joy in them that I increasingly
    set my heart "on things above" (Colossians 3:1).
Thank you for the assurance you give that we are your children
    (Romans 8:16).
Thank you for the gift of your Spirit, "freely given" to me
    (1 Corinthians 2:12).
Thank you for the "surpassing worth" of knowing you, Jesus,
    for you are the greatest blessing of all (Philippians 3:8).
"Every spiritual blessing!" I'm "an heir" to everything good (Galatians 4:7),
    even though I'm entirely unworthy of it.
How amazing you are to love me and die for me.
You demonstrated your love for me when you were the furthest thing
    from my mind (Romans 5:8).
Father, just as you've had mercy on me and blessed me beyond imagination,
    I'd like to ask for your mercy and blessing for
    my child.
Just as "Isaac blessed Jacob and Esau in regard to their future" (Hebrews
    11:20), I'd like to ask for future blessings for my son.

I ask that he will be transformed by the renewing of his mind
to know you and love you (Romans 12:2).
Change his mind and heart with your "treasures of wisdom and knowledge"
(Colossians 2:3) so that he wants you more than anything else.
Touch his stubborn will with your "perfect love" that drives out fear
(1 John 4:18).
May your peace, "which transcends all understanding" (Philippians 4:7),
rest upon him as he turns his back on the world and draws near to you.
I know you want to bless him too, Father!
Let him live in such a way that he may be truly blessed by you.
"As a father has compassion on his children,
so the LORD has compassion on those who fear him" (Psalm 103:13).
Thank you for the blessing of your compassionate, fearless love, Lord Jesus.
I praise you, because you "have overcome the world" (John 16:33).
You are "God who saves" (Psalm 68:20).
Bless him with your salvation, Lord, just like you have blessed me.
Then together we will "praise you forever;
from generation to generation" (Psalm 79:13).

———

Imagine that your prodigal is before you and reach out your hand as if it is on his or her head. Then pray for God's best blessings, starting with a heartfelt relationship with Jesus.

DAY 77

Through All Generations

Your faithfulness continues through all generations.

PSALM 119:90

Thank you for always being faithful, Lord.
I praise you for the promise of your unshakeable love:
"Though the mountains be shaken and the hills be removed,
yet my unfailing love for you will not be shaken" (Isaiah 54:10).
"O Lord God, you are God!
Your words are true" (2 Samuel 7:28 esv).
"Your word, Lord, is eternal" (Psalm 119:89).
It's for future generations that I ask your help, Father, starting with
my daughter.
When I look at the direction the world is going,
I'm reminded that "the heart is deceitful above all things
and beyond cure" (Jeremiah 17:9).
But you are "the Lord, who heals" (Exodus 15:26).
So, like the parents who brought their children to you,
I ask you to touch her, Lord Jesus (Matthew 19:13).
She is not as close to you as she needs to be, so I ask you to
use the situations in her life right now to turn her to you.
Place your people in her path, Father,
and let her be drawn to them in ways she cannot explain.
Let her see so-called coincidences and understand that they are much
more than that, because you are at work to capture her heart.

Let her see you moving wherever she goes,
因为 because "the earth is full" of your "unfailing love" (Psalm 33:5).
I pray that she will no longer be "captive to sin" (Acts 8:23),
but that she will freely give her heart to you in love.
As I think about her future, Father, I'd also like to pray for the man
she will one day fall in love with and marry.
I ask that you will be at work in his life as well,
to save him and show him your way.
I pray that their marriage will be established in your unconditional love,
and that you will be welcomed into their home in every way.
I also pray for any children you would give them, and for grandchildren,
great-grandchildren, and beyond, that "from the lips of children
and infants," you would ordain praise (Matthew 21:16).
I praise you too, Father, because "nothing is too hard for you"
(Jeremiah 32:17).
Because you are faithful from generation to generation,
you are entirely able to answer this prayer,
and I praise you for what you will do!

**Ask for God to bless generations of your family so they may follow Him,
and praise Him for being faithful!**

Everything Is Possible

When the spirit saw Jesus, it immediately threw the boy into a convulsion.
He fell to the ground and rolled around, foaming at the mouth.
Jesus asked the boy's father, "How long has he been like this?"
"From childhood," he answered. "It has often thrown him into
fire or water to kill him. But if you can do anything, take pity
on us and help us." "'If you can'?" said Jesus. "Everything is possible
for him who believes." Immediately the boy's father exclaimed,
"I do believe; help me overcome my unbelief!"

MARK 9:20-24

"If you can do anything . . ."

Those words weren't exactly filled with hope. The man who said them to Jesus had tried everything he could think of for his son. Even Jesus's disciples had not been able to help the boy (Mark 9:18).

Jesus is quick to respond: "If you can? . . . Everything is possible for him who believes."

The man jumps hungrily at the thought: "I do believe; help me overcome my unbelief!"

I love that prayer. I've found myself praying it more than once.

When you're the parent of a prodigal, you find your faith challenged in many ways. Sometimes your child challenges what you believe. Other times, you may find yourself struggling when answers to prayer don't come as quickly as you may have hoped.

It's comforting that Jesus didn't rebuke the father for his plea for help with his unbelief. He answered the plea with action. Jesus exercised his spiritual authority and commanded the demon to leave the man's son (Mark 9:25).

In the moment before Jesus spoke to free the man's son, the man's faith hadn't changed. He still had his questions and doubted whether something could be done. He was honest about his struggles and lack of faith, and Jesus met that transparency with kindness.

Even the smallest amount of faith placed in Jesus's hands can move mountains (Matthew 17:20). We need to give not only the situation that weighs so heavily on us to him, but ourselves as well.

Later Jesus's disciples "asked him privately, 'Why couldn't we drive it out?'" Jesus answered, "This kind can come out only by prayer" (Mark 9:28–29). Earlier the disciples had been given "authority over impure spirits" (Mark 6:7). Jesus had sent them out, and they "drove out many demons and anointed many sick people with oil and healed them" (Mark 6:13). So why couldn't they do it this time?

The answer lies in their question. Jesus said that apart from the Father, He could "do nothing" (John 5:30). But the disciples asked: "Why couldn't *we* drive it out?" Their focus was no longer on God's authority and his ability to answer prayer, but on themselves.

Sometimes we pray after we've tried everything else and nothing has seemed to work. Jesus's answer shows that instead we need to make prayer our "first resort" and not our last.[11] Then, we will discover that His power is "made perfect in weakness" (2 Corinthians 12:9).

When by faith we take hold of Jesus, reaching for Him and not just what He can do for us, He *takes hold* of us and lifts us to new places of grace. When we give up control and long for His authority over our lives and the lives of our children, depending on him with new prayerfulness, we discover the hope that "everything is possible for him who believes."

We may have our questions and struggles, but that doesn't change who Jesus is. We can "cast all" our "anxiety on him because he cares for" us

---

11. Banks, *Lost Art of Praying Together*, 24.

(1 Peter 5:7). His words to the struggling father that day are the same to the parents of prodigals today: "Bring the boy to me" (Mark 9:19).

> *We have to pray with our eyes on God, not on the difficulties.*
>
> —OSWALD CHAMBERS

A Larger Lion

Be alert and of sober mind. Your enemy the devil prowls around
like a roaring lion looking for someone to devour.

1 PETER 5:8

I see lion tracks, Lord. Right behind him.
The tracks have been close for a while now. Too close.
My son has been walking in the enemy's territory, and he's in danger.
He's being stalked every step he takes, but he doesn't see it.
Help him, Father! "You alone, LORD,"
    make him "dwell in safety" (Psalm 4:8).
I pray that you will protect him.
Let him look around the road that he's on and see that it leads nowhere.
I ask that you turn him around
    so his feet will no longer "rush into evil" (Proverbs 1:16).
I pray he will "turn from evil and do good,"
    and "seek peace" with you (Psalm 34:14).
Save him, Father! "Come quickly" to his "rescue" (Psalm 31:2).
Even though the enemy pursues him, I ask that you,
    "the Lion of the tribe of Judah," be swifter still (Revelation 5:5).
Let your love overtake him and protect him every step he takes.
    "I look for your deliverance, LORD" (Genesis 49:18).
When the enemy attacks my son, I pray that you "will fight for" him,
    before his "very eyes" (Deuteronomy 1:30).
I praise you that with you on his side, my son faces a defeated foe.

In the moment that you deliver him, may he hear you speaking to his soul: "I am the LORD, and there is no other; apart from me there is no God. I will strengthen you, though you have not acknowledged me" (Isaiah 45:5).

You say in your Word, Father, that you "will lead the blind by ways they have not known, along unfamiliar paths" you "will guide them;" you "will turn the darkness into light before them and make the rough places smooth" (Isaiah 42:16).

My son needs you to lead him in that way, Lord. Out of the dark and into the "everlasting light" of your presence so that his "days of sorrow will end" (Isaiah 60:20).

Those "who walk in the light of your presence" are blessed (Psalm 89:15), and I want my son to know your blessing!

"Come, Lord Jesus" (Revelation 22:20), come soon to give my son the grace he needs.

Come into his life in a fresh and powerful way so he will surrender his heart to you!

————

God told Cain, "Sin is crouching at your door; it desires to have you" (Genesis 4:7). Pray that your prodigal will strongly desire to turn away from sin and run to the Lord for a new beginning.

Long in the Land

Children, obey your parents in the Lord, for this is right. "Honor your father and mother"—which is the first commandment with a promise—"So that it may go well with you and that you may enjoy long life on the earth."

EPHESIANS 6:1–3

Father, I ask that you will help my daughter to live in such a way
that she may be blessed.

You promise that those who "honor" their "father and mother" *will* be
blessed: it will "go well" with them, and they will "enjoy long life on
the earth."

She's struggling with honoring her parents right now. She thinks that
obedience will lead to a lack of life, instead of one that is better.

Thank you, Father, for the reminder that children are to obey their parents
"in the Lord."

I'm not up to the job of parenting without you!
"Apart from you I have no good thing" (Psalm 16:2).

I praise you that with you I will have all that I need, not only to meet the
challenges of parenting a child who is rebelling, but also to overcome
those challenges.

Your Word gives me this assurance: "Who is it that overcomes the world?
Only the one who believes that Jesus is the Son of God" (1 John 5:5).

I *do* believe in you, Lord. And I thank you that you will get us through this
difficult time.

I pray that you will help my daughter learn to obey even when
it isn't easy.

Help her to see that obedience doesn't mean that she is weak.

Instead, it's a sign of strength of character.

I pray that you will help me to obey you too, Lord.

Obedience to you is the best way to show you that I love you,

because "this is love for" you: to obey your commands (1 John 5:3).

Father, I pray that my daughter will also be obedient to you so she

"will be blessed" in every way (John 13:17).

Let her love you and follow you!

Give her insight to see that when she walks in the world's ways,

she is simply conforming to the world and *obeying* it,

and there is no freedom or originality in that.

Give her grace to understand that "we must obey" you

"rather than human beings" (Acts 5:29).

It is only through you that she can discover her true identity,

all that you uniquely created her to be.

Give me grace as well, Father, for those moments

when I face my daughter and our wills collide.

I pray "your will be done" (Matthew 26:42) fully and freely in both of our

lives, because those who do your will, you promise, will live in your

land "forever" (1 John 2:17)!

———

Pray that your prodigal will come to understand that love for God leads to obedience to Him.

Sitting in the Courtroom

If you, LORD, kept a record of sins, Lord, who could stand?
But with you there is forgiveness, so that we can, with reverence, serve you.

PSALM 130:3-4

He's in trouble, Lord, and he needs your help.
He's up against circumstances so much bigger than he is,
    and he doesn't yet understand the consequences of his actions.
But you love him, and that's my greatest hope.
I hold on to your Word: "But God demonstrates his own love for us in this:
    While we were still sinners, Christ died for us" (Romans 5:8).
You saw this coming and still loved him with the greatest love imaginable
    (John 15:13).
He needs that right now. More than any attorney,
    he needs you to be his "advocate" (Job 16:19).
"Let him return to the LORD, so he may have compassion on him,
    and to our God, for he will freely forgive" (Isaiah 55:7 CSB).
It is your mercy he needs more than anything else.
Not just for what he stands accused of, but for his heart and soul.
Use this, Lord. Use this experience to change his heart
    so that you may "have mercy" on him (Romans 11:32).
Let your kindness lead him "to repentance" (Romans 2:4).
Let the "godly sorrow" that "brings repentance that leads to salvation
    and leaves no regret" turn his heart entirely to you
    (2 Corinthians 7:10).
Everything in me wants to help him, if only I could.

I know that the best help I can give him is to bring him
and everything about this situation to you in prayer.
I pray that when we're sitting in the courtroom,
we will not be afraid because you go with us, and you "will never leave"
us "nor forsake" us (Deuteronomy 31:6).
I pray that when my son stands before the judge, he will be reminded that
"we will all stand before God's judgment seat" (Romans 14:10).
I ask that my son will be respectful and will answer wisely,
saying only what you would have him say (see Proverbs 16:1).
I pray that he will "submit to governing authorities"
and not rebel in any way (Romans 13:1–2 NLT).
I pray as well for the judge, that you will give him "the wisdom that comes
from heaven" (James 3:17) and that he will be "God's servant" to do
my son "good" (Romans 13:4).
I pray that you will move in the judge's heart to accomplish your purposes
and that mercy will triumph "over judgment" (James 2:13).
I pray all of this in the strong name of Jesus, who stood accused for me
(Matthew 27:12) that I may go free (John 8:36).

————

Pray that your prodigal will bow his or her heard before God as the one, true "righteous judge" (Psalm 7:11) and cry out to Him for the help He alone can give.

Should Have, Would Have, Could Have

If only you had paid attention to my commands,
your peace would have been like a river,
your well-being like the waves of the sea.

ISAIAH 48:18

I know someday she'll have her regrets, Lord.

I'd like to send this prayer on ahead to that time.

One day she will look back on her life and wish she had done things differently.

She will regret the difficult things that passed between us and feel a hurt in her heart, because of the love you've given us for each other.

On that day, Lord, because you are the one "who comforts us in all our troubles" (2 Corinthians 1:4), I ask that you quiet her with your love.

I pray that she will know your presence and the peace you alone can give to those who walk with you as their Lord and Savior.

I ask that you will "speak tenderly" to her
    and tell her "that her sin has been paid for" (Isaiah 40:2).

Thank you, Father, that we can bring all of our should-haves, would-haves, and could-haves to you and find healing and hope.

I pray you will turn her around from the road that leads only to regret and draw her heart to you.

I praise you, Lord Jesus, that with you new beginnings are possible every day.

With you, we can "press on toward the goal" of heaven and hope
(Philippians 3:14).
We need not "long for the months gone by" (Job 29:2),
because you are always with us.
You even have the future completely under control.
We need not fear tomorrow, because you are already there!
You hold time in your hands.
Lord, you "wash away all my iniquity and cleanse me from my sin"
(Psalm 51:2).
I pray that your grace will reach my daughter in the same way so she
can turn her back on the past and look to you with confidence.
Let her hear you say to her, "Forget the former things; do not dwell on
the past" (Isaiah 43:18).
I pray that she will repent of her sins and know that she is completely forgiven.
Your Word promises, "If anyone is in Christ, the new creation has come:
The old has gone, the new is here!" (2 Corinthians 5:17).
I pray that she will "be glad and rejoice forever" in what you will create
(Isaiah 65:18), that you may be her joy,
and that she will be yours.

———

Luke 1:78 speaks of God's "tender mercy" to us in Jesus. Pray that your
prodigal will long for that mercy deeply in her or his heart.

Everything She Ever Wanted

The fruit of that righteousness will be peace;
its effect will be quietness and confidence forever.

ISAIAH 32:17

If she walks with you, Father, it changes everything.
She will "have peace" in you (John 16:33),
    because you are "our peace" (Ephesians 2:14).
She will have every blessing she needs, because in your grace you
    never take your "eyes off the righteous" (Job 36:7).
What a full and beautiful life you have planned for her, Lord!
Father, I pray she will hear the promptings of your Holy Spirit telling her,
    "In repentance and rest is your salvation,
    in quietness and trust is your strength" (Isaiah 30:15).
Let her repent of her sins and find peace with you!
Because "there is no one righteous, not even one" (Romans 3:10),
    I pray for the righteousness only you can give, which is "righteousness,
    peace and joy in the Holy Spirit" (Romans 14:17).
Clothe her "with garments of salvation" (Isaiah 61:10),
    because "all our righteous acts are like filthy rags" (Isaiah 64:6).
If she asks you for wisdom, you "[give] generously to all without finding
    fault!" (James 1:5).
I pray that she will ask and "will receive"
    so that her "joy will be complete" (John 16:24).
You are complete joy, Lord! Please help her to make that discovery.
Then she will find everything she ever wanted in all that you are.

I pray that she will come to "the full measure of the blessing of Christ" (Romans 15:29) and become a blessing to others!

If she comes to you and remains in you, she will "bear much fruit" (John 15:5).

I also ask that she will be fruitful by pointing others to you.

May she "bear fruit—fruit that will last" (John 15:16), and "still bear fruit in old age" (Psalm 92:14).

Let her share the story of what you have done for her with confidence to all who will listen!

But first, let her discover your "incomparably great power for us who believe" (Ephesians 1:19).

O Father, let today be the day!

———

Ask God to help your prodigal discover the unexpected joy that comes from turning away from our sins and turning to Him.

In All Things, God

*And we know that in all things God works for the good of those
who love him, who have been called according to his purpose.*

ROMANS 8:28

It amazes me, Father, how you waste nothing.

You are sovereign over every single experience of life.

You use it all—the happy times and the heartbreaking ones—to bring
good that you alone can give.

As I look back on my life with my child, Lord,

I think of how I imagined it very differently.

I didn't expect the challenges we've faced together,

and I know that she doesn't bear responsibility for all of them.

I know I've made mistakes too, Lord.

Thank you for your mercy and grace that meet us both right
where we are.

She needs it to open her eyes and turn her "darkness to light"
(Acts 26:18).

I need it to remind me of your "everlasting love" (Jeremiah 31:3),

and that even though I stumble, I "will not fall,"

because you hold me up with your hand (Psalm 37:24).

I praise you, Lord, for the unexpected mercies along the way—

good things that I didn't expect that were clearly from your hand.

How true it is that your "compassions never fail.

They are new every morning" (Lamentations 3:22–23).

Thank you for your fresh mercy that meets us every day, Father!

Thank you for "the incomparable riches" of your grace that you want to
show us in your "kindness to us in Christ Jesus" (Ephesians 2:7).
There are good days ahead as we turn to you. Help us to do it, Lord!
Your Word promises that "those who fear the LORD are secure";
you "will be a refuge for their children" (Proverbs 14:26 NLT).
My child needs your refuge, Lord, and "the shelter of your presence"
to keep her safe (Psalm 31:20).
"You, Lord, are forgiving and good, abounding in love
to all who call to you" (Psalm 86:5).
I call on you, Father, because "no one can fathom"
your greatness (Psalm 145:3).
I call on you, Lord Jesus, because you "have overcome the world"
(John 16:33).
I call on you, Holy Spirit, because you search
"even the deep things of God" (1 Corinthians 2:10).
You alone, Lord, can bring us safely through the storm.
How faithful you are to your promises,
and how loving you are to us (Psalm 145:13).
I stand on your Word today: "I sought the LORD, and he answered me;
he delivered me from all my fears" (Psalm 34:4).
I praise you that you are a God who "richly blesses all who call" on you
(Romans 10:12).

———————

**Praise God that His love for you and your prodigal is deeper and more
compassionate than anyone can comprehend.**

River of Delights

How priceless is your unfailing love, O God!
People take refuge in the shadow of your wings.
They feast on the abundance of your house;
you give them drink from your river of delights.

PSALM 36:7–8

A "river of delights." What a beautiful thought!
Show my son the way to that river, Lord.
Let him dive in headfirst and discover "how wide and long and
    high and deep is the love of Christ" (Ephesians 3:18).
I can see him splashing around in it, his face a picture of joy.
Let him drink of its sweet, refreshing water
    and "never thirst" again (John 4:14).
I pray that you will satisfy every longing of his soul.
You are the true source of every delight,
    "the spring of living water" (Jeremiah 17:13).
"Every good and perfect gift" comes from you (James 1:17).
You say in your Word, "Let the one who is thirsty come;
    and let the one who wishes take the free gift of the water of life"
    (Revelation 22:17).
You promise that "to the thirsty" you "will give water without cost from
    the spring of the water of life" (Revelation 21:6).
He is thirsty, Lord. But right now he doesn't understand that only you
    can quench his thirst.
I ask that he will understand, and the sooner, the better.

Good Shepherd, I ask you to lead my son to the clear,

"quiet waters" of your peace, and there restore his soul (Psalm 23:2–3).

He's swum in the devil's sewage long enough.

"Wash" him, and he "will be clean" (Psalm 51:7).

Just as you are "able to guard what I have entrusted" to you (2 Timothy
1:12), grab him by the hand and pull him up from the world's deadly
and filthy undertow.

Save him, Lord! Breathe into him the breath of eternal life.

Show him the beautiful, pure person you intend him to be,

filled with your Spirit and with your love.

May your "righteousness" roll on "like a never-failing stream," Savior
(Amos 5:24).

I praise you for "the river of the water of life, as clear as crystal,

flowing from the throne of God and of the Lamb" (Revelation 22:1).

Let him be lifted by your water of life and carried to new places of grace.

Then he will show others the way to the river too, because "rivers

of living water will flow from within" (John 7:38).

And together we'll swim in your joy forever!

———

"Take delight in the Lord" (Psalm 37:4 NLT). For a moment simply sit in
His presence and love Him. Then pray that your prodigal will come to
know the depth of joy He gives.

God's Timing

Jesus told [the synagogue ruler],
"Don't be afraid; just believe."

MARK 5:36

Sometimes God doesn't give us what we're asking for so he can give us what we really want.

That's what happened to Monica. For more than nine years, she prayed for her son Augustine to come to Christ. She prayed with such passion that a bishop in their city told her, "It is not possible that the son of these tears should perish."[12]

But as Monica prayed, her son wandered further and further from God. When she learned that he wanted to leave their home in North Africa to sail to Rome, the center of vice and corruption in her time, she became distraught and followed him all the way to the harbor where the ship was waiting.

Then he tricked her.

Augustine told her he could not leave until a friend was ready to sail. He suggested she get some rest that night at a chapel beside the harbor. While she was sleeping, he left. She looked out on the harbor the next morning to discover that the ship had sailed and her son with it, *the very thing she was praying would not happen.*

---

12. Augustine, *Confessions*, 3.12, available at ccel.org/ccel/augustine/confess.iv.xii.html.

But it was in Rome that Augustine would give his heart to God. His life would be transformed forever, and God would use Augustine's faith to inspire generations to believe in Jesus.

Augustine later recalled the evening he left his mother in his book *Confessions*: "The wind blew and swelled our sails, and withdrew the shore from our sight; and she on the morrow was there, frantic with sorrow, and with complaints and groans filled Thine ears, Who didst then disregard them." He concludes insightfully, "Thou, in the depth of Thy counsels and hearing the main point of her desire, regardest not what she then asked, that Thou mightest make me what she ever asked."[13]

When the very thing you're praying won't happen *does*, it's easy to become discouraged.

I have to wonder how Jairus felt. He came to Jesus and "fell at his feet. He pleaded earnestly with him, 'My little daughter is dying. Please come and put your hands on her so that she will be healed and live'" (Mark 5:22–23). While they were on the way to Jarius's home, a woman who was chronically ill pressed through the crowd and touched Jesus. "At once Jesus realized that power had gone out from him. He turned around in the crowd and asked, 'Who touched my clothes?'"

If I were Jairus, I would be thinking, *My daughter is* dying, *and you're stopping in a* crowd *to ask a question like that?* Even the disciples wondered aloud, "You see the people crowding against you . . . yet you can ask, 'Who touched me?'"

Jesus not only stopped, He *kept waiting*. "Jesus kept looking around to see who had done it. Then the woman, knowing what had happened to her, came and fell at his feet and, trembling with fear, told him the whole truth."

For Jairus, this meant more delays. Then men from his house showed up, and they were hardly compassionate: "'Your daughter is dead,' they said. 'Why bother the teacher anymore?'"

Jesus ignored them. He told Jairus, "Don't be afraid; just believe."

---

13. Augustine, *Confessions*, 5.8, available at ccel.org/ccel/augustine/confess.vi.viii.html.

You know how the story ends. Jesus went to Jairus's house, and the mourners laughed at Him. He threw them out and brought the girl back to life (Mark 5:22–43).

Praying for a prodigal will stretch your faith. What can help in the especially difficult times is to remember that God's timing is rarely our own. Things may seem to go from bad to worse, but He has complete authority over the situation. When it seems like hope is lost, it only means God isn't finished yet.

Sometimes we wonder why we keep praying. In those times, it's good to remember that the heartless and laughing voice of doubt never has the last word. That word belongs to God. Jesus moves at His own pace, and He is never late. His advice to a worried parent long ago still speaks to us today: "Don't be afraid; just believe."

God is faithful, and He will answer our prayers in His perfect timing and wisdom. His Word reminds us that His ways and thoughts are "higher" than our own (Isaiah 55:9). He is never flustered or delayed, and nothing can stop Him from carrying out His purposes. Though we may not be able to see Him coming, that doesn't mean that He isn't about to show up in a life-giving way that changes everything for the better. Just around the corner, we may bump into the grace God intended all along.

The joyful discovery Jairus and Monica made is ours to make as well. Hope isn't lost. It is only taking another way.

When I am dealing with an all-powerful, all-knowing God,
I, as a mere mortal, must offer my petitions not only with
persistence but also with patience. Someday I'll know why.

—RUTH BELL GRAHAM

DAY 85

Those Who Are with Us

"Don't be afraid," the prophet answered. "Those who
are with us are more than those who are with them."
And Elisha prayed, "Open his eyes, LORD, so that he may see."
Then the LORD opened the servant's eyes, and he looked and
saw the hills full of horses and chariots of fire all around Elisha.

2 KINGS 6:16-17

When I try to wrap my mind around all that you are, Lord,
    I am simply astounded.
Your Word tells me of "thousands upon thousands of angels in joyful
    assembly" around you (Hebrews 12:22).
You said of our children that "their angels in heaven always see"
    the Father's face (Matthew 18:10).
How wonderful you are, Lord!
"What is mankind that you are mindful of them?" (Psalm 8:4).
You are "majestic in holiness, awesome in glory, working wonders"
    (Exodus 15:11).
It helps to keep that in mind. Sometimes it seems like my child and
    I are up against things that seem so much bigger than us.
The times that we live in, the culture, the media—all of these things
    affect our lives in ways beyond our control.
But I praise you that they are not beyond yours!
I thank you that one day "every knee should bow, in heaven and on
    earth . . . and every tongue confess that Jesus Christ is Lord"
    (Philippians 2:10–11 RSV).

You are Lord over every challenge we face, and all of history is heading in
your direction, "Judge of all the earth" (Genesis 18:25).

Lord Jesus, I thank you that "trouble or hardship or persecution or famine
or nakedness or danger or sword" shall not "separate us" from your love
(Romans 8:35).

My son needs your love, and he needs to know you.

Right now he is impressed with "the ways of this world" (Ephesians 2:2),
which are "passing away" (1 Corinthians 7:31).

"O LORD, open his eyes so he may see."

Just as you opened the eyes of Elisha's servant, I pray that you will help my
son to see that "there is none like you" (Psalm 86:8).

Give him grace to understand that he wants to be on your side,
because "those who are with us are more than those
who are with them."

One day, you will bring all of history to a close.

I pray we will both be ready on the day that you return, Lord Jesus!

Then we will look "forward to a new heaven and a new earth, where
righteousness dwells" (2 Peter 3:13), where "the earth will be filled with
the knowledge of the LORD as the waters cover the sea" (Isaiah 11:9).

**Thank the Lord that there is no problem or situation in your prodigal's life
that He is not greater than.**

DAY 86

For Strength to Love

Who shall separate us from the love of Christ? Shall trouble or hardship
or persecution or famine or nakedness or danger or sword?

ROMANS 8:35

"I love you, LORD, my strength" (Psalm 18:1).

I love you because you've "freely given" me your grace (Ephesians 1:6).

You loved me even before "the creation of the world" (Ephesians 1:4).

When I was completely lost and "dead in transgressions,"
    you loved me and gave me life (Ephesians 2:4–5).

You are love, Lord (1 John 4:16). "Your love is better than life" (Psalm 63:3).

Your "love compels" me (2 Corinthians 5:14).
    I want to live in your love, Lord.

Over every virtue I want to "put on love" (Colossians 3:14).

I want to live with faith and hope and love,
    "but the greatest of these is love" (1 Corinthians 13:13).

"Love never fails" (1 Corinthians 13:8).

I want others to sense your love in me before I even say a word.

Especially my son.

My son is a gift and blessing from you. I love him so much, Father!

But as much as I love him, you love him even more.

Your love is perfect! Your love is "from everlasting to everlasting" (Psalm
    103:17).

He needs your love so much.

Love through me, Lord! Let your love flow through me to draw
    him to you.

I know what love is because you've showed it to me through the
way you "laid down" your life and loved me so sacrificially (1 John 3:16).
Father, give me grace to love like you do.
I ask for the strength to love him when it isn't easy.
Help me to love him enough to be patient with him,
because "love is patient" (1 Corinthians 13:4).
Help me to speak "the truth in love" (Ephesians 4:15)
and share your Word with him.
When he does something wrong, help me to love him enough to discipline
him "because the Lord disciplines the one he loves" (Hebrews 12:6).
When he does something right, let me be the first to praise him,
because love "rejoices with the truth" (1 Corinthians 13:6).
Father, you are "slow to anger, abounding in love
and forgiving sin and rebellion" (Numbers 14:18).
I want to love him like that, with a love that "always protects, always trusts,
always hopes, always perseveres" (1 Corinthians 13:7).
I choose to love, Father, just as you chose to love me.
Fill me afresh with your Spirit, so that I can
"do everything in love" (1 Corinthians 16:14).
Make my love "increase and overflow," Lord (1 Thessalonians 3:12),
for you and for my son, that he may one day praise you for it and love
you with all his heart, soul, mind, and strength (Mark 12:30).

**Sit with your head bowed and your hands open on your lap, and ask the Lord
to pour His love into you afresh (see Romans 5:5).**

DAY 87

Hiding Place

You are my hiding place;
you will protect me from trouble
and surround me with songs of deliverance.

PSALM 32:7

I remember when we used to play hide-and-seek. We had so
much fun!
She used to love to be found. I'd pick her up in my arms,
hold her close, and we'd both laugh together.
I have that picture in my mind of you, Lord.
You took children in your arms and "blessed them" (Mark 10:16).
I ask that you do that for my daughter once again.
You are the Good Shepherd, who "gathers the lambs in his arms
and carries them close to his heart" (Isaiah 40:11).
She needs your touch, Lord (Luke 18:15).
She needs you to take her by the hand and lead her "along the right paths"
for your name's sake (Psalm 23:3).
When she was little, she would try to hide by covering her eyes,
as if that were enough.
That's not unlike what she's trying to do now, Father,
even though you see her "every step" (Job 34:21).
I remember the times that I've tried to hide from you, but in your kindness
you made me understand: "Where can I go from your Spirit? Where
can I flee from your presence?" (Psalm 139:7).
Nothing in all creation is hidden from your sight (Hebrews 4:13).

I pray that you will open her eyes that she "may know the hope" to which you have called her (Ephesians 1:18).

I pray that she will no longer run *from* you, but run *to* you, because you have set her heart free (Psalm 119:32).

I pray that you will be her "hiding place," Father. Then you will protect her from trouble and surround her with "songs of deliverance" (Psalm 32:7), just as you have me.

May she "take refuge" under your wings (Ruth 2:12) and hear the still, small voice of your Spirit in a "gentle whisper" telling her she is loved (1 Kings 19:12).

"Make your face shine upon" her, dear Lord, to restore her and save her in every way (Psalm 80:3 NASB).

Then she will "find delight in the Almighty" and lift her face to you (Job 22:26). Her face will shine with your light and your love, because those who look to you are "radiant; their faces are never covered with shame" (Psalm 34:5).

Pray your prodigal will one day know the joy of the "glorious freedom" (Romans 8:21 NLT) of a relationship with God through Jesus.

DAY 88

Always There

And surely I am with you always, to the very end of the age.

MATTHEW 28:20

"He was always there for me" is one of the best things that can be said
about a parent.

I pray that my daughter will one day say that about me, Father.

I thank you and praise you that I can say that about you!

Wherever I go, your wonderful Spirit goes with me:

"If I go up to the heavens, you are there;

if I make my bed in the depths, you are there" (Psalm 139:8).

I am never alone. You draw close to me in your kindness,

and bless me with "your presence forever" (Psalm 41:12).

If I went to the other side of the world or even the deepest region of space,

"even there your hand will guide me, your right hand will hold me

fast" (Psalm 139:10).

What could matter more than simply being with you?

What could I possibly need "besides you" (Psalm 73:25)?

There is "one thing I ask" of you, Lord (Psalm 27:4).

As blessed as I am to know that you are with me always and that I will

one day be with you, I long for my child to love you too.

Your Word says that "the children of your servants will live in your

presence; their descendants will be established before you"

(Psalm 102:28).

"Truly I am your servant, Lord" (Psalm 116:16)

because of your kindness and grace!

I pray that my daughter will live in your presence in heaven and in the
kingdom to come by first coming to faith in you on this earth.

May she know in her heart that our love for her, strong as it is,
pales in comparison with yours!

All love comes from you. Your Word even says, "Though my father and
mother forsake me," you "will receive me" (Psalm 27:10).

Thank you for holding out your arms for her, Lord Jesus.

May there be no doubt that she has received you,
so that you may receive her forever.

"To all who believed" you and "accepted" you
you "gave the right to become children of God" (John 1:12 NLT).

I pray that right will be hers, Father, and I give her to you again today.

She is my child, but I want her to be yours as well, just as you made *me*
your child through your incredible mercy in Jesus.

———

**Thank the Lord for His promise that "I am with you always" (Matthew
28:20 ESV), and pray that your prodigal will know the peace of His presence
in his or her heart.**

He Is Yours, and So Am I

*"I am the Lord's servant," Mary answered. "May your word
to me be fulfilled." Then the angel left her.*

LUKE 1:38

Mary's response was amazing, Father.

After the angel told her news that would turn her life upside down,
    she simply said, "I am the Lord's servant."

She didn't ask, What will Joseph say when he discovers I'm pregnant?
    Or, What will people think?

She just gave herself and her son to you.

I want to do the same thing, Father.

I know that he is better off in your hands than mine.

But it isn't easy. He is *my* son, but he is also *your gift.*

Because I love him, I want to protect him.

    I want to keep him from pain and harm.

The thought of giving him up in any way goes straight to my soul.

I remember what Simeon told Mary:

    "A sword will pierce your own soul too" (Luke 2:35).

I can't imagine what Mary went through, seeing her own son crucified.

But *you* went through the same thing, Father! He was *your* son too.

That is the very thing that gives me hope and lets me know that it's safe to
    give my son to you: "He who did not spare his own Son, but gave him
    up for us all—how will he not also, along with him, graciously give us
    all things?" (Romans 8:32).

Forgive me for being possessive, Lord.

How can I not give you my son when you have given yours to me?

So I pray with your Son, my Savior,

"Not my will, but yours be done," Father (Luke 22:42).

I place my son in your hands. He needs you more than anything else.

Because you "graciously give us all things" (Romans 8:32), I ask that you give him grace to receive you so that he may "be filled to the measure of all the fullness of God" (Ephesians 3:19).

I ask that he will "consider everything a loss because of the surpassing worth of knowing Christ Jesus" (Philippians 3:8).

You said it yourself, Lord: "What good is it for someone to gain the whole world, yet forfeit their soul?" (Mark 8:36).

Thank you, Father, for the peace that comes when I bow not just my head, but my heart to you as well.

In my heart, I "worship Christ as Lord" of my life (1 Peter 3:15 NLT), and thank you for the blessing that will come.

———

Our heavenly Father tells His people in Isaiah 43:1 (ESV), "I have called you by name, you are mine." Thank the Lord that you belong to Him, and pray that your prodigal will hear God calling him or her, and respond.

DAY 90

I Believe

We live by faith, not by sight.

2 CORINTHIANS 5:7

I believe, Father.

I believe that you want me to pray for my child because my prayers will make a profound difference for good in her life.

I believe that you gave her to me for a reason that has more to do with your vision for her eternity than my wishes for her on this earth.

I believe that you want me to be "wrestling in prayer" for her (Colossians 4:12) so that through prayer, things will change for the better.

No matter what the situation looks like now or what other people may say, no matter what conventional, earthly wisdom may forecast for her future, I will believe *you.*

I will seek you above all others,

because "you have the words of eternal life" (John 6:68).

I believe you are even better than I know, and are at work in ways that I cannot see.

So I will "live by faith, not by sight" and always hold on to hope.

"And this hope will not lead to disappointment" because you have been kind to us and "have given us the Holy Spirit to fill our hearts with" your love (Romans 5:5 NLT).

Like Jacob wrestling, "I will not let you go unless you bless me" (Genesis 32:26), and I praise you that you will never let *me* go,

because you have said, "Never will I leave you; never will I forsake you" (Hebrews 13:5).

I will persevere for my daughter with prayer after prayer until she realizes
how much you love her.

Oh, how I want my daughter to love you, Lord!
And I believe that one day she will—fully, freely, joyfully!

I believe, Lord, because your Word tells me that "without faith it is
impossible to please" you, because anyone who comes to you must
believe that you exist and that you reward those who earnestly
seek you (Hebrews 11:6).

I believe you will reward me as I seek you with all of my heart,
and you will bless my daughter as she turns to you.

I believe that the future you have in store for her is beautiful—
filled with "grace and peace" (1 Peter 1:2).

I believe because in your great mercy you have already given me
"new birth into a living hope through the resurrection of Jesus Christ
from the dead" (1 Peter 1:3).

Because you are the "hope of glory" (Colossians 1:27), Jesus, and you are
in me, my hope will live always: today, tomorrow,
and forevermore!

———————

**Ask God to increase your faith in all He is able to do to one day bring your
prodigal home to Him.**

Conclusion

Prayer moves the hand that moves the world.

—E. M. BOUNDS

William didn't have time for his mother's Christian faith. Though she spoke with him frequently about Jesus and he often caught her praying for his salvation, he kept going his own way.

Before she died, she gave him a Bible.

He sold it when he needed some extra cash.

Still, William was what you might call a "successful" prodigal. He graduated from medical school and began working as a physician in a hospital.

One day, a man was brought in who had been in a serious accident on the job. William did his best to help him, but it was clear that the man would soon die from his injuries. William broke the news to him as best he could.

The man had two requests. He asked to see his landlady so he could pay his rent, and he requested she bring him his Bible.

In the days that followed, he kept the Bible close. He read it as long as he could. When he no longer had the strength to hold it, he kept it under his covers. He died a short time later.

A nurse was cleaning his room after his death and found the Bible. "What shall we do with this?" she asked William, handing it to him.

William's own words recount what happened next:

I took the Bible and—could I trust my eyes? It was my own Bible! The Bible which my mother had given me when I left my parents' home, and which later, when short of money, I sold for a small amount. My name was still in it, written in my mother's hand. . . .

With a deep sense of shame I looked upon . . . the precious book. It had given comfort and refreshing to the unfortunate man in his last hours. It had been a guide to him into eternal life, so that he had been enabled to die in peace and happiness. And this Book, the last gift of my mother, I had actually sold for a ridiculous price. . . .

Be it sufficient to say that the regained possession of my Bible was the cause of my conversion.[14]

William's mother never saw her prayers for her son answered on earth, but she did see them answered in heaven. Through her prayers and faith, God used her to reach her son years after her life in this world was over. She placed her trust in Him, and He showed himself faithful. After all, He is the One who promised, "In this world you will have trouble. But take heart! I have overcome the world" (John 16:33).

"Take heart!" We need to hear those words from Jesus again and again. Jesus said them often.

As he bent over a young man stricken with paralysis, he told him, "Take heart, son . . ." (Matthew 9:2).

When a chronically ill woman reached out to touch his coat, he whispered, "Take heart, daughter . . ." (Matthew 9:22).

God hears our prayers for our prodigal sons and daughters and *will* show himself faithful. Even when the challenges seem insurmountable, we can *take heart* because He holds the world in His hands. Even when the answers to our prayers seem long in coming, they are on the way.

That brings us back to William.

Dr. William P. Mackay eventually left medicine and became a minister. God used him to inspire many through his books and hymns. His best-known hymn, "Revive Us Again," shows a passionate and faithful heart filled with a contagious love for his Maker:

> *We praise Thee, O God, for Thy Spirit of light,*
> *who has shown us our Savior and scattered our night.*
> *Hallelujah! Thine the glory! Hallelujah! Amen!*
> *Hallelujah! Thine the glory! Revive us again!*

I have a feeling that when he wrote those words, his mother must have been smiling.

14. Quoted in Morgan, *Then Sings My Soul*, 147.

For Group Discussion and Prayer

This thirteen-week study was developed to help encourage people who are reading *Prayers for Prodigals* together. All you will need is the book and your Bible. There are six questions for each week, drawn from the reflections and the prayers. There are also instructions for praying for your prodigals together. For more helpful information about forming a prodigals prayer group, visit the "Prayer Resources" page at JamesBanks. org. And while you're there, be sure to visit the "Prodigal Prayer Wall," and also drop James a note and let him know you are doing this study. He loves to encourage groups as they pray.

WEEK 1

1. In the introduction, James writes, "God blessed me with two prodigals. I use the word *blessed* because they are a gift, just like every child." What is one thing that you love about your prodigal—perhaps something about the way God made him or her—that you are thankful to God for?

2. This thought is also in the introduction: "Prodigals are an especially precious gift because they teach us much, including patience, the depth of our own need for forgiveness, and continued dependence on God in prayer." What have you been learning through the experience of having a prodigal in your life? Has it caused you to pray more? Why or why not?

3. The parents of prodigals can sometimes feel like no one understands. The reflection for Week 1 describes the depth of Jesus's compassion when He encounters the widow from Nain and tells her, "Don't cry" (Luke 7:13). How does it help you to understand that Jesus not only understands but also has compassion for you and your prodigal?

4. The prayer from Day 1 communicates the truth from 2 Thessalonians 2:16 that God offers us "eternal encouragement and good hope." How does this thought challenge or encourage you as you bring your prodigal before Him in prayer?

5. Day 3 addresses facing "the giant of rebellion" in a prodigal's life. Discuss together how God is greater than any obstacle you face in your prodigal's life.

6. Day 7 quotes Psalm 63:7, "Because you are my help, I sing in the shadow of your wing." What practical action will you take to rest in God's love and power this week?

Praying Together: Begin by reading Psalm 63:1–8, and finish one of these sentences as you pray together: "Lord, you are my help because . . ." or, "I sing (or rest) in the shadow of your wing because . . ." If you have a need you would like the group to pray for, share it by simply praying it briefly (as you tell God, you are also telling others). Conclude your time in prayer as a group by thanking God that He is greater than any obstacle you may face in your prodigal's life and by looking forward in faith to what He will do in answer to prayer.

WEEK 2

1. E. M. Bounds wrote, "Only God can move mountains, but faith and prayer can move God." Mark 10:14 uses a word that is used nowhere else in the New Testament to describe how Jesus felt about something. What was the word, and why did Jesus feel that way? What does this tell us about His response to our desire to bring our loved ones before Him in prayer?

2. In the reflection for Week 2, James writes that "even 'successful' kids can be prodigals, and Christian parents who have them have to be careful not to be lulled into a false sense of security." Discuss this statement together in light of Jesus's words in Mark 8:36–37.

3. In Luke 15:2 the Pharisees muttered about Jesus, "This man welcomes sinners and eats with them." What does this tell us about the kind of people Jesus spent time with and about His heart for our prodigals?

4. In "The Son of These Tears" (Day 9) James writes, "I believe one reason you've given my son to me is so I can pray for him to have the joy of knowing you forever." How might the thought that God has blessed you with children for His own eternal purposes affect the way you pray for them?

5. How would you feel if you heard Jesus saying "Bring the boy to me" (Mark 9:19) or "Bring the girl to me" to you about your prodigal? What comfort and hope does it give you to know that He wants you to do this through faithful and honest prayer?

6. Day 14 ("If I Should Die before She Wakes . . .") brings up the truth that because of God's mercy, our prayers may "outlive" us. What encouragement does this give you as you pray for your prodigal?

Praying Together: In Psalm 34:1 David writes, "I will bless the Lord at all times; his praise shall continually be in my mouth" (ESV). Praising God as we begin to pray helps to encourage our faith in Him before we bring our requests before Him. Spend the first several minutes together praising God by praying any of His attributes or names (do this before you pray for the needs in your prodigals' lives). Remember to use brief prayers so as many as possible can participate.

WEEK 3

1. Matthew 20:20–28 tells us about the mother of James and John and her awkward request of Jesus. What was the request? Do you agree with the thought that her sons probably put her up to it? Have you ever been pulled into one of your prodigal's schemes without fulling knowing what was going on (see Matthew 20:22)?

2. The reflection for Week 3 discusses our tendency to keep score and compare ourselves with others: "When you're the parent of a prodigal child, you may feel like you have to settle for second best when it comes to the future." Still, God wastes nothing, and He is able to use even the difficult choices our loved ones have made for later good in their lives. Together, discuss the importance of seeking God's ultimate goals for our children instead of our own.

3. What hope does God's showing favor to Joseph in prison (Genesis 39:20–21) or to Daniel in exile in Babylon (Daniel 1:9) give you for your prodigal, even when he or she is in a difficult place?

4. "God of the Second Chance" (Day 19) looks at Jesus's reinstatement of Peter after Peter denied Him. What does Jesus's giving Peter a new beginning tell you about His heart for those who have strayed? Discuss this in light of God's desire for "all people to be saved and come to a knowledge of the truth" (1 Timothy 2:4).

5. James begins Day 20 with the words, "Something good is coming, and I thank you for it, even though I don't know what it is yet! But I know *you*." Lamentations 3:23, which describes God's compassion as "new every morning," was written in a time of crisis for Israel. How does the description of God's character given in this verse offer you hope as you go through difficult times?

6. Imagine Jesus telling you to "take heart" as you pray for your prodigal. How does the truth that He has "overcome the world" (John 16:33) give you peace and hope regarding any obstacles you face with your prodigal?

Praying Together: Revelation 5:8 describes "golden bowls full of incense, which are the prayers of God's people" kept before God in heaven. This shows us how God treasures our time before Him in prayer. Begin by thanking Him together for this, and then intercede for your prodigals. Remember to simply bring your requests for your prodigals directly before God instead of talking about them as a group, as this maximizes time spent together with Him in prayer.

WEEK 4

1. In Luke 15:20 Jesus uses the words "while he was still a long way off" to describe where the prodigal's son was when his father saw him. What does this show us about God's heart for those who are distant from Him and His understanding of our challenges with our prodigals?

2. In "The Running Father," the reflection for Week 4, James writes, "No one cares more about prodigals than Jesus. Jesus loves my prodigal son and welcomes my prayers for him. Jesus wants to restore him to the Father and welcome him home. He has called me to join in His search and rescue mission. Together, we're going after my son." How does it help to know that Jesus loves your prodigal even more than you do and that He shares your desire to see your loved one return to Him?

3. Discuss J. Sidlow Baxter's quote: "Our loved ones may spurn our appeals, reject our message, oppose our arguments, despise our persons—but they are helpless against our prayers."

4. What is your favorite promise from God's Word that encourages you as you pray for your prodigal? (Note the Scripture verses in Day 26, "You Promised!")

5. First Thessalonians 5:18 instructs us, "Give thanks in all circumstances, for this is God's will for you." This can be challenging when we're going through difficult seasons, but it also helps us remember to place our hope in God. What are you thankful for right now?

6. In Genesis 28:16 Jacob says, "Surely the LORD was in this place, and I was not aware of it." Discuss how knowing that God can be at work in your prodigal's life in ways you do not comprehend can give you hope as you pray for him or her (see Day 28, "Blessed without Knowing It").

Praying Together: Read 1 Corinthians 13:4–7, and begin by praising God for His love. (You might use a prayer starter such as, "Your love is precious to me because . . ." and finish the sentence with an attribute from the verses you just read.) As you pray today be sure to spend time together confessing sins before God (either aloud or silently), and ask for strength to forgive and let go of any "record of wrongs" with your prodigal.

WEEK 5

1. In the reflection for Week 5 "Stretchers of Faith," James writes about the impact of his mother's faith on his life. Is there someone whose faith made a difference for you?

2. Mark 2:5 and Luke 5:20 give us Jesus's response to those who brought a man to Him to be healed: "When Jesus saw *their* faith . . ." We don't know about the faith of the man who was healed, but we do know the faith of others made an impression on Jesus. Discuss what this can mean for those who pray for their prodigals together.

3. In 2 Chronicles 20:12 King Jehoshaphat tells the Lord as he prays with others about an approaching army, "We do not know what to do, but our eyes are on you." How is this a helpful perspective in the struggles we face with our prodigals? Where do you need to keep your eyes on the Lord and trust Him more, instead of looking at the circumstances alone?

4. In the prayer for Day 31 ("Whoever"), James quotes the promise of John 3:16 that "whoever believes in" Jesus "shall not perish but have eternal life." How does the word "whoever" give you hope for your prodigal?

5. Two prayers from this week talk about "A Better Attitude" (Day 32) and "A Softer Heart" (Day 30). How does it encourage you to know that God can change your prodigal's heart and attitude, and your own as well?

6. In "Innocence Found" (Day 34), James contrasts the concept of "innocence lost" with a new beginning in Christ. Together, discuss the difference Jesus can make in a heart and life as we become a "new creation" in Him (2 Corinthians 5:17).

Praying Together: Begin by praising God together for the difference He makes in our lives (Colossians 1:13). Then take turns praying for each other's prodigals one at a time by name, lifting each one on a "stretcher of faith" together. Be sure to conclude your prayer time with prayers that look forward in faith to what God alone can do.

WEEK 6

1. The reflection for Week 6, "Just Say the Word," considers a Roman centurion's response to Jesus's authority over a need in his life (Matthew 8:5–13). What insight does the man have about Jesus? Together, discuss Jesus's response to his faith.

2. Day 36 ("For Chains to Fall") starts with Psalm 107:14 and God's power to break away chains. Talk together about some of the chains you've seen God break in hearts and lives when someone turns to Jesus.

3. Day 37 ("For an Honest Answer") is a plea for honesty in relationship with our prodigals. When Geoffrey Banks was struggling with substance abuse, he would sometimes ask James, "Don't you trust me, Dad?" and James would respond, "I *want* to trust you" (he couldn't respond fully with a "yes"). Can you relate to that answer? (You can read more about Geoffrey and James's story in their book, *Hope Lies Ahead*).

4. The prayer "Off Broadway" (Day 38) contrasts our entertainment choices with Jesus's words, "Broad is the road that leads to destruction" (Matthew 7:13). Discuss together how an unhealthy focus on our own entertainment can distract us from the kingdom of God.

5. In Day 41 ("For Freedom from Substance Abuse") James writes, "I can see him set free, Lord. Shining from head to foot, smiling and strong, a living example of your kindness and love." Discuss the importance of being able to see our prodigals not just as they are but as they *can be* with God, as we pray for them.

6. The prayer "Praise for Small Victories" (Day 42) considers Zechariah 4:10 and the importance of faith in God in seemingly minor circumstances. Discuss why this matters, and (if you like) share any small victories you have seen in your prodigal's life.

Praying Together: A man told Jesus in Mark 9:24 (NLT), "I do believe, but help me overcome my unbelief." Begin by praising God through completing this prayer starter together: "Lord, I believe in you because. . . (name some of His attributes, or what He has done)." Then, take a time of silence to ask for His help with any unbelief in your heart and life. Then name any chains you would like to see fall in your prodigal's life or in your own (just a word or two will do). Conclude by praising God for any small victories that you've seen or that are to come!

WEEK 7

1. In this week's reflection, "Coming to Our Senses," James shares the story of the encouragement God gave his grandmother in a very difficult time in her life. Discuss any special encouragement you have received from God either recently or in the past.

2. This week's reflection also points out that "God uses our prayers to pull us close and show us what He alone can do." Discuss how praying for our prodigals helps both *us* and our prodigals.

3. Day 45 ("Songs in the Night") contains these words: "I always thought things like this happen to other people." Day 48 ("Praise in the Dark") considers the hope that God gives as we persevere in prayer through challenging times. Why is it helpful to find our comfort and strength in God, praising His goodness regardless of our circumstances?

4. The prayer for Day 46 ("Accepting Rejection") looks at some of the hard decisions we sometimes have to make with our prodigals. Together, discuss how it must have felt for Jesus to face the rejection of those He loved and the importance of staying close to Him as we seek to love our prodigals back to God.

5. Day 47 ("When Distance Separates") brings up the vital truth from Isaiah 59:1 that there is nowhere our prodigals can go where God cannot reach them. Talk about any times when you have seen God reach someone under improbable circumstances.

6. The prayer for Day 49 ("Constant Help") addresses the description of God from Psalm 46:1 as an "ever-present help in trouble." What does it mean to you that you can turn to God—regardless of what is happening—wherever you may be? How are you doing with "declaring your dependence" on Him as you walk this road with your prodigal?

Praying Together: Begin by praying the first verse of Psalm 46 and one of these prayer starters: "You are my strength because . . ." or, "You are my ever-present help because . . ." Then pray for your prodigals by name. Have someone read verse 10 and sit quietly before God for a moment. Conclude with a time of thanking the Lord that He is always "with us" (see Psalm 46:7, 11), no matter what our circumstances may be.

WEEK 8

1. In "Treasured in Our Hearts," James mentions some moments with his daughter that he cherishes. Did your prodigal have faith as a child? What were some of your favorite moments?

2. Day 51 ("Light His Feet") addresses how God uses His living Word to transform our hearts and lives. What Scripture verses have you found particularly encouraging as you pray for your prodigal?

3. In Day 52 ("Shame Off Her!") James writes, "I pray my daughter will understand that when prodigals return, you throw a party! You welcome them with arms held wide open!" Discuss how we might encourage our prodigals to feel loved and welcomed so that they turn to Jesus.

4. "Straight Steps" (Day 54) is about the importance of God's wisdom in our lives. James 1:5 tells us, "If any of you lacks wisdom, you should ask God, who gives generously to all without finding fault." Where do you need wisdom right now with your prodigal?

5. Day 54 also contains this prayer: "Place wise people in his path that he will listen to." Discuss the importance of praying for wise friends for our prodigals, and for ourselves as well.

6. Day 56 ("Inexhaustible") brings up the topic of God's inexhaustible love, which renews us "day by day" (2 Corinthians 4:16). Discuss some of the aspects of the strength that God is able to give us as we draw near to Him in prayer.

Praying Together: Begin by having someone read Psalm 23, and praise God for any aspects of His character listed there. As you pray for your prodigals by name, be sure to note that His goodness and love *follow* us (see Psalm 23:6—this word can also be translated "pursue") as long as we live.

WEEK 9

1. In "Waiting for an Answer" James writes about the painful experience of his daughter running away and how that taught him and his wife, Cari, to move at God's pace instead of their own. How can staying close to God through prayer and His Word help us discern His leading?
2. The reflection for Week 9 also mentions the encounter between Jesus and the Canaanite woman who came to Him for her daughter. Part of that encounter is difficult, especially when "Jesus did not answer a word" (Matthew 15:23). Why is it important to keep praying for our prodigals even when God seems silent?
3. Jesus eventually tells the woman, "Your request is granted" (Matthew 15:38). Discuss any encouraging progress you may have seen with your prodigals as you have prayed for them.
4. The prayer "Back to Flame" (Day 59) includes an encouraging description found in Isaiah 42:3 (read the verse aloud together). What does this tell us about the Lord? How does knowing this help you as you continue to pray for your prodigal?
5. Go around the room reading the verses from Ephesians 6:10–18 (addressed on Day 60 in the prayer "Dressed in Armor"). What vital part of the armor of God is usually never shown in illustrations? (Hint: see v. 18).
6. Discuss Jesus's words in Luke 15:10 (see Day 61, "When Angels Sing"). What hope does that verse give you as you pray for your prodigal?

Praying Together: Start by reading Zephaniah 3:17 and praising God with the prayer starter, "You are mighty to save because . . ." Then pray for your prodigals one by one, and after each name repeat the words, "You are mighty to save."

WEEK 10

1. The reflection for this week ("Who Sinned?") considers the disciples' question for Jesus about a man who was blind from birth: "Rabbi, who sinned? This man or his parents, that he was born blind?" (John 9:2). What was Jesus's answer? What does His response show us?

2. Have you ever felt like God was "paying you back" through your prodigal for things you had done in the past? Discuss this together, in light of Jesus's response to the disciples in John 9:30 and God's promise in Ezekiel 18:20.

3. Note in the account of Jesus healing the blind man in John 9 that the blind man did not ask for help; Jesus voluntarily went to him. How can this give us hope for those we love who are spiritually blind and cannot see Him yet? How does Romans 5:8 affirm this truth?

4. The prayer from Day 65 ("Strength to Go On") begins with this striking assertion from Habakkuk that despite a number of negative things happening in his life, "Yet I will rejoice in the Lord, I will be joyful in God my Savior" (Habakkuk 3:18). Why is this a vital choice to make when we are going through difficult times?

5. Day 67 ("When You're, 'Prayed Out,'") begins with the honest assertion, "Sometimes I feel too numb to pray, Father." Have you ever felt that way, as if you are going over the same ground again and again without any progress as you pray for your prodigal? What hope does Romans 8:34 give you under these circumstances?

6. The prayer from Day 70 ("More Than I Ask or Imagine") considers what God is able to do in response to our prayers. What hopeful message does Ephesians 3:20–21 give us about this?

Praying Together: As you begin, take turns reading aloud through Paul's prayer in Ephesians 3:14–21. Then apply the requests made in that prayer to your prodigals as you pray for them. Conclude by rejoicing in God (remember Habakkuk?) and praising Him for what He is able to do. For additional encouragement, agree to pray Ephesians 3:14–21 for each other this week.

WEEK 11

1. The reflection from Week 11 ("The Good Shepherd") looks at God's search and rescue mission for us and our prodigals. What does the response of the shepherd to finding his sheep (see Luke 15:5–6) tell us about Jesus's heart for the lost?

2. In the same reflection, James writes about Jesus, "Even though His sheep has strayed, he or she could be close, just over the next hill. The Good Shepherd knows, and He has a way of surprising us." Sometimes we imagine it will take decades for our prodigals to come home instead of a much shorter time, but God is able to do anything. Discuss this together, and talk about the need to stay close to Him regardless of how much time it takes.

3. The prayer for Day 71 ("Your Dream for My Child") contrasts God's desires for our children with our own. Discuss why is it important for us to want what God wants for them and to yield to His wisdom in this.

4. Day 73 ("The Contender") looks at the efforts of our adversary, the devil, as he tries to draw our loved ones away from God. Discuss this in light of the truths of 1 Peter 5:8–9 and Jesus's promise to us in John 16:33.

5. "Running to Jesus" (Day 74) lifts up several aspects of Jesus's identity. Talk about some of the scriptural names of Jesus found in this prayer and talk about how they can help us as we pray for our prodigals.

6. Day 76 ("Every Blessing") delves into how God has "given us every spiritual blessing in Christ" (Ephesians 1:3), and brings up the subject of blessing children. Together, talk about some of the ways we might ask God to bless our loved ones even while they are on a prodigal path.

Praying Together: As you begin your prayer time, thank God for the blessings of belonging to Jesus (any you can think of). Follow up on those thoughts by asking God for those same blessings for your prodigals as you pray for them by name.

WEEK 12

1. This week's reflection ("Everything Is Possible") looks at Jesus's conversation with a distraught father in Mark 9:20–24, who tells Him, "But if you can do anything, take pity on us and help us." What does Jesus say in response to that statement? What is the man's response to Jesus after that?

2. In this reflection James writes, "Even the smallest amount of faith placed in Jesus's hands can move mountains (Matthew 17:20)." Why is this helpful to keep in mind as we pray for our prodigals?

3. Discuss this thought from the reflection: "Sometimes we pray after we've tried everything else and nothing has seemed to work. Jesus's answer shows that instead we need to make prayer our 'first resort' and not our last." Do you think the human tendency to make prayer an afterthought might have been behind the disciples' private question to Jesus in Mark 9:28–29?

4. The prayer for Day 78 ("A Larger Lion") contains these words: "I praise you that with you on his side, my son faces a defeated foe." Why is this important to keep in mind as we pray for our prodigals? How does it strengthen our faith?

5. Day 80 ("Sitting in the Courtroom") addresses an issue often faced by those who love prodigals. What are some of the ways we can pray for those who face legal challenges? Is there anyone who needs prayer in your group right now?

6. "In All Things, God" (Day 83) begins with the words, "It amazes me, Father, how you waste nothing." Have you seen an instance in your or your prodigal's life where God took something difficult and used it to bring about an unexpected good?

Praying Together: Begin by reading Romans 8:28 before prayer time, and praise God for anything you like (nothing is too big or too small). Then lift up the needs in your prodigals' lives, thanking God that He is able to use even the most difficult circumstances for good. Continue by having someone read Romans 8:31–39, and conclude by looking forward in faith to what God will do in answer to prayer.

WEEK 13

1. This week's reflection ("God's Timing") examines what God did in Augustine's life in answer to his mother's prayers. How long did Monica pray for her son before he came to Christ? How do you think she must have felt when the very things she was praying wouldn't happen did happen?

2. The reflection begins with these words: "Sometimes God doesn't give us what we're asking for so that he can give us what we really want." This thought is based on Augustine's statement about what happened that day (found later in the reflection). Why is this actually a comforting thought as we pray for our prodigals?

3. Mark 5:22–43 tells us about the synagogue leader Jairus coming to Jesus with an urgent request for his daughter, but something happens and Jesus is delayed along the way. What might this incident—and the daughter's subsequent healing—reveal about God's timing and our prayers?

4. "He is Yours, and So Am I" (Day 89) demonstrates an effort to give our prodigals to God—something that can be difficult to do. How does the truth expressed by Romans 8:32 give us comfort and hope as we do this?

5. Day 90 ("I Believe") begins with the words of 2 Corinthians 5:7: "We live by faith, not by sight." Why is this a helpful verse to keep in mind as we pray for our prodigals? James writes, "I will persevere for my daughter with prayer after prayer until she realizes how much you love her." Why is perseverance in prayer important? (hint: see Hebrews 11:6).

6. The conclusion of *Prayers for Prodigals* tells the story of Dr. William Mackay, a "successful" prodigal who would eventually turn to Jesus. What means did God use to bring him "home"?

Praying Together: Begin by reading the hymn lyrics (written by William Mackay) that are quoted at the end of the conclusion, and spend some time praising God together in any way you like. After you pray for your prodigals, read Romans 8:32 aloud and thank God for His faithfulness as you persevere in prayer. Conclude by having someone read Philippians 4:6–7 aloud.

Resources for Those Who Love Prodigals

WEB

JamesBanks.org. James's personal site. Parents may enter anonymous requests for their children on the "Prodigal Prayer Wall" at this site. Please also visit the "Prayer Resources" page and use the search feature for "Praying for Prodigals" for additional resources and video interviews with James and Geoff.

BOOKS

On Prayer and Parenting

Prayers for Your Children, James Banks. Our Daily Bread Publishing.

Prodigals (and Those Who Love Them), Ruth Bell Graham. Baker Books.

Biographies/Autobiographies

The Girl in the Song, Chrissy Cymbala Toledo. Tyndale Momentum.

Rebel with a Cause, Franklin Graham. Thomas Nelson.

Come Back, Barbara, C. John Miller and Barbara Miller Juliani. P & R Publishing.

Out of a Far Country: A Gay Son's Journey to God, A Broken Mother's Search for Hope, Christopher Yuan and Angela Yuan. WaterBrook Publishing.

Recovery/Addiction Related

Addictions: A Banquet in the Grave, Edward T. Welch. P & R Publishing.

Holy Sexuality and the Gospel, Christopher Yuan. Multnomah Books.

Tell Your Children: The Truth about Marijuana, Mental Illness, and Violence,
Alex Berenson. Free Press.

The Secret Thoughts of an Unlikely Convert, Rosia Champagne Butterfield.
Crown and Covenant.

Sources

Augustine, Aurelius. *The Confessions of St. Augustine*. Translated by Edward B. Pusey. Oak Harbor, WA: Logos Research Systems, Inc., 1999. Available at Christian Classics Ethereal Library, ccel.org/ccel/augustine/confess.i.html.

Banks, James. *The Lost Art of Praying Together*. Grand Rapids: Discovery House, 2009.

Bounds, Edward McKendree. *The Complete Works of E. M. Bounds on Prayer*. Grand Rapids: Baker, 1990.

Chambers, Oswald. *Prayer: A Holy Occupation*. Grand Rapids: Discovery House, 1992.

Chesteron, Gilbert Keith. *Orthodoxy*. Garden City, NY: Image Books, 1959.

Cymbala, Jim. *Fresh Faith*. Grand Rapids: Zondervan, 1999.

————. *Fresh Wind, Fresh Fire*. Grand Rapids: Zondervan, 1997.

Faber, Frederick William. *Growth in Holiness*. Baltimore: John Murphy and Company, 1855.

Graham, Ruth Bell. *Prodigals and Those Who Love Them*. Grand Rapids: Baker, 1999.

Morgan, Robert J. *Moments for Families with Prodigals*. Colorado Springs NavPress, 2003.

————. *Then Sings My Soul*. Nashville: Thomas Nelson, 2003.

Newton, John, and William Cowper. *Olney Hymns*. London: W. Oliver, 1797.

Pascal, Blaise. *Pensees*. Translated by W. F. Trotter. Christian Classics Ethereal Library, ccel.org/ccel/pascal/pensees.i.html.

Prime, Samuel. *The Power of Prayer*. Edinburgh: The Banner of Truth Trust, 1991.

Spurgeon, Charles Haddon. *The C. H. Spurgeon Collection*. Rio, WI: Ages Software, 1998–2001.

Index

anger, Day 5, Day 43

anxiety, Day 4, Day 45

attitude, Day 32

beauty: inner, Day 75

blessing, Day 76, Day 82, Day 84

choices, Day 54

committing child to God, Day 89

confession of faith, Day 90

consequences, Day 8

deliverance, Day 6; from hell, Day 29; from temptation and sin, Day 16

discernment, Day 57; in media choices, Day 38

encouragement, Day 1

Enemy, the, Day 73

failure, Day 2

faith: rekindled, Day 59

fear, Day 23

forgiveness, Day 18, Day 22

friends, Day 33

future, Day 17, Day 53, Day 68; day of salvation, Day 69; generations, Day 77; plans, Day 11, Day 71; regrets, Day 81; spouse, Day 55

God: His power, Day 3; His promises, Day 26; His sovereignty, Day 83

grace, Day 25

heart, Day 30, Day 72

home: far from home, Day 47; hasn't come home, Day 50

honesty, Day 37

honor toward parents, Day 79

intercession, Day 9

Jesus: power of His name, Day 74

legal difficulties, Day 80

love, Day 86

manipulation, Day 44

opportunity, Day 15

patience, Day 66

perseverance, Day 67

power: transformative, Day 10

praise, Day 7, Day 20, Day 21, Day 48, Day 63, Day 65, Day 70, Day 85, Day 87; for angels, Day 62; for blessing, Day 28; for ever-present help, Day 49, Day 88; for innocence, Day 34; for prayer, Day 13, Day 14; for small victories, Day 42; for strength, Day 56; of thanksgiving, Day 27; for understanding, Day 35

profanity, Day 39

protection, Day 60, Day 78

rejection, Day 46

restoration, Day 12

salvation, Day 31, Day 58, Day 61

Scripture, Day 51

second chance, Day 19

service, Day 24

sexual immorality, Day 40

shame, Day 52

sin: habitual, Day 36; of the parents, Day 64

substance abuse, Day 41

About the Author

Dr. James Banks has a gift for encouraging others to pray. James is the author of several books and a writer for the *Our Daily Bread* devotional as well as blogs, magazines, radio broadcasts, and podcasts. His writings have been translated into multiple languages to bring help and hope to readers around the world. His recent book, *Hope Lies Ahead* (Our Daily Bread Publishing 2020), is a follow-up to *Prayers for Prodigals*. Coauthored with his son, Geoffrey, who is now a youth pastor, *Hope Lies Ahead* chronicles specific answers to prayer made over a period of years, and it offers a candid look at how Geoffrey was rescued out of heroin addiction by coming to faith in Jesus Christ.

A graduate of Westmont College, James holds advanced degrees from Princeton Theological Seminary and Gordon-Conwell Theological Seminary where he received the Servant of the Kingdom Award for his ongoing work furthering prayer in the Church. The church he founded and still pastors, Peace Church in Durham, North Carolina, is a growing congregation with a priority on helping others discover a prayer-filled relationship with Jesus Christ.

Married for thirty-nine years, James and his wife, Cari, have two children and two grandchildren. James loves taking time off with his family, walking along the river with his Labrador retriever pal, Max, and tinkering under the hood of a car.

James is a popular speaker at church events, conferences, and retreats. For information about having James speak at your event and to view his most recent projects, visit JamesBanks.org.

Spread the Word
by Doing One Thing.

- Give a copy of this book as a gift.

- Share the QR code link via your social media.

- Write a review of this book on your blog, favorite
  bookseller's website, or at ODB.org/store.

- Recommend this book to your church, small
  group, or book club.

Our Daily Bread

Connect with us. [f] [◎] [𝕐]

Our Daily Bread Publishing
PO Box 3566, Grand Rapids, MI 49501, USA
Email: books@odb.org